W9-BOY-613

<u>What the Experts Are Saying</u>

"This book should be available to every family who must deal with the consequences of violent crime in America."

Sue Holtkamp, Ph.D., Director, Something More Bereavement Programs

"The direct style and approach of the book seems to cut through a lot of the myth and murkiness that must surround traumatic loss. I find it also offers helpful guidelines for caregivers who desire to be responsibly attentive to the victims of a traumatic loss."

David Miller, Pastor, Church of the Brethren

"A needed and invaluable source of practical, insightful information for both survivors of homicide victims and the professionals who work with them. I would like to see every newly bereaved family receive one as the notifying officer leaves the home."

Jean Lewis, National President, Parents of Murdered Children, Inc.

" I highlighted something on nearly every page."

A Bereaved Mother

"It is of course a sad comment on American life that a book like this is 'popular' ... [b]ut what a relief to know that when something like this is needed, Jenkins is the guy who wrote it."

Pat Holt, Reviewer, Holt Uncensored

"... truly a one of a kind offering that should be available through any victim's rights group or law enforcement agency. It fills the need of practicality with compassion for anyone experiencing a loss through a murder, suicide, accidental death, or any other type of traumatic death."

Trudy Weathersby, Reviewer, About.com – Death and Dying

"This book will answer a lot of your questions ... A violent death leaves many victims in its wake. That's the unfortunate reality."

Kay Scarpetta in Patricia Cornwell's novel, *The Last Precinct*

"... a blueprint, which can help survivors rebuild their lives. Only someone who has experienced a personal tragedy could be so effective in providing this kind of support and guidance to survivors ... the help you need to carry on, when there is no other place to turn."

Bob Wallace, P.I.O., Chief of Police Magazine

"Jenkins' courage and vision in writing the book can be of help to the many people who will face the unexpected loss of a loved one."

Editorial, Carroll County Times, Maryland

"You never know when a friend or loved one is going to need this book to pull them through ... something that is sorely needed by thousands of persons who have had to endure the experience of losing a loved one. It is also essential reading by others in order that they have some idea of what a family truly goes through when crime strikes."

Jerry Pearce, The Radio Detective, KMPH-FM

"This book's audience is far greater than most would expect. It's a fine resource for anyone affected by violent crime – health-care workers as well as victims' family and friends."

Devlin Donaldson, Reviewer, CBA Marketplace

"An excellent book."

Countless Victim Advocates

Finalist – Best First Book by a New Author

Publishers Marketing Association, Benjamin Franklin Awards 2000

"[Jenkins] embraces the reality by offering friendly, insightful and encouraging directions, redirections and, at times, resurrection or rescue for families and individuals who now must work through systems and snares to come to terms first with the reality of the violence in loss and the justice system issues that follow and then, finally, to 'begin' their sorrowful outpouring."

Rev. Dr. Richard Gilbert, World Pastoral Care Center

"It is an excellent practical way to assist families of homicides, suicides, car crashes and other tragic accidents. It is written by someone who has had that visit from a police officer at a late hour. He has felt the pain, searched for answers and realized others needed as much help as he did."

Stephen Palmer, Yellow Book News for Funeral Directors

"[A] useful resource, suitable for many types of situations and losses. It is a much needed tool for those who are confronted with the traumatic loss of their loved one. ... This book should be made available to every family who must deal with the consequences of violent crime in Canada and the United States."

Patricia Simone, Cardinal Funeral Homes

"I would have given almost anything to have had this book available to my family and me in 1990 when my sister was murdered."

Jennifer Bishop, Murder Victims Families for Human Rights

WHAT TO DO WHEN THE POLICE LEAVE:

A Guide to the First Days of Traumatic Loss

Third Edition

Bill Jenkins

 WBJ Press

Chicago, IL

The poem *Remember Me* is reprinted with the permission of Bereavement Publications, 5125 N. Union Blvd., Suite 4, Colorado Springs, CO 80918

Quotations at the beginning of each chapter are from the author's personal writings, all other quotes are used with permission or are in the public domain.

The mention of any company or organization in the text does not necessarily imply an endorsement of materials or services, merely their availability.

For information on ordering copies of this book at quantity discounts, or to provide comments or feedback contact:
http://www.willsworld.com

Publishing History:

First Edition	August, 1998
Second Edition	June, 1999
Third Edition	January, 2001

10 9 8 7 6 5 4 3
Printed in the United States of America

Publisher's Cataloging-in-Publication
(Provided by Quality Books, Inc.)

Jenkins, Bill, Prof.
    What to do when the police leave : a guide to the
first days of traumatic loss / Bill Jenkins. -- 3rd ed.
    p. cm.
    Includes bibliographical references.
    LCCN: 00-109793
    ISBN: 0-9667600-1-8

    1. Murder victims' families--United States--
Psychology. 2. Grief. 3. Bereavement.   I. Title.

HV6529.J46 2001   155.9'37
                        QBI00-899

Dedication

This work is lovingly dedicated
to the memory of my son,
William Jenkins,
and to loved ones everywhere who are victims of
violence in our communities, streets, and homes.
It is our fervent hope and prayer that someday
books such as this will be obsolete,
that the courtrooms and prisons will stand vacant,
and that the police will have no need to patrol our streets.
For in that day, we will all take upon ourselves
the responsibility to enforce peace, respect, and kindness
in our world for the good of all.

William Benjamin Jenkins
September 16, 1980 - August 12, 1997

17th Homicide Victim of 1997,
Henrico County, Virginia

Hope

In desperate hope I go and search for her in all
the corners of my room; I find her not.

My house is small and what once has gone from
it can never be regained.

But infinite is thy mansion, my lord, and
seeking her I have come to thy door.

I stand under the golden canopy of thine
evening sky and I lift my eager eyes to thy face.

I have come to the brink of eternity from which
nothing can vanish – no hope, no happiness, no
vision of a face seen through tears.

Oh, dip my emptied life into that ocean, plunge
it into the deepest fullness. Let me for once feel
that lost sweet touch in the allness of the universe.

Rabindranath Tagore,
from *Gitanjali*, LXXXVII

Table of Contents

Foreword _____ *5*

Preface _____ *7*

"What Do We Do Now?" _____ *9*

The Checklist _____ *11*
    Eight Things You Need to Know Right Now

Your Local Victim Assistance Program _____ *15*

First Things First _____ *17*
    The Checklist in Detail •
    Emergency Response and Crime Scene Cleanup

Funerals and Funeral Homes _____ *47*
    Planning a Funeral on Short Notice

Grief and Grieving _____ *55*
    Men and Women in Grief • Grief "Stages" •
    A Few Words About Acceptance •
    Roadside and Other Memorials • Grief in the Workplace •
    Getting Support • What You Can Do Now •
    Some Physical and Emotional Effects of Grief and Anxiety

Children and Grief _____ *77*
    How Children Understand Death

Grief Responses _____ *87*

**The Notification • Placing Blame • Homicide • Suicide •
Tragic Accident • Religious Responses**

The Police and Criminal Justice System _____ *107*

**The Investigation • The Unsolved Case • The Trials •
The Civil Justice System**

Long-Term Grief -- Living the Marathon _____ *127*

**Vulnerability • Grieving and Growing •
Living the Marathon**

Conclusion _____ *137*

Appendix:

Organizations and Resources_____ *139*

    Organizations • Internet Resources

Annotated Bibliography_____ *145*

    Books • Magazines • Brochures

Victim and Witness Rights _____ *153*

How to Help a Friend in Grief _____ *155*

    Information to Share With Others

*Author's Note*_____ *159*

Acknowledgments _____ *161*

Contact Numbers _____*166*

It is very easy to see the allure of alcohol to dull the pain and the temptation to punish myself for something that is not my fault. But the sobering truth is that if I step onto the path of self-destruction, I know I will never come back.

A Random Thought During the Holidays

Foreword

I wish I could say that the brutal, cold-blooded murder of Will Jenkins is the only heartless, senseless tragedy I have ever been exposed to in my sixteen years of working in a medical examiner's system and doing intensive research in every aspect of violent, sudden, and unexpected death.

What has always struck me deeply over the years is that tragedy strikes swiftly like an earthquake and there is no long-term follow-up in the news or even in social programs that intimately reveals or adequately copes with the long-term devastation to those left behind. It was not uncommon when I was a computer analyst at the medical examiner's office in Richmond for me to do a name search in the case database and have several of its surnames roll up on my screen. As I pulled those cases I would find that, for example, a woman was raped and murdered one year, then several years later her father committed suicide, and some time after that, the mother died of chronic alcoholism. A violent death, as we say in the morgue, takes out everyone around it.

Those left behind are grief-stricken, stunned, and finally caught up in a system they neither prepared for nor understand. What *do* you do when the police leave and the attention moves on to the next case, the next day on the job for those who do the autopsies and the forensic tests and conduct the funerals? How do you survive the first days of traumatic loss and the impending grief and emptiness that you know will sear your soul for the rest of your life? How do you deal with the funeral homes or the sudden isolation of finding that people, even your friends, either avoid you or approach you with voyeuristic inquisitions? Then there are the endless interviews by detectives and district attorneys and the probes in depositions that violate every aspect of the life of the victim, the family, and all who knew him or her. Finally, there is the trial or the stormy sessions with insurance companies and the relentless inquiries by the media, and finally, silence as the world forgets.

On August 12, 1997, sixteen-year-old Will Jenkins, a handsome, honorable young man, was shot to death by a robber using an illegally obtained handgun. It was Will's second day at his first "real" job at a fast food restaurant. For the first time, someone left behind – his father, Bill Jenkins – has taken the time and summoned up the courage to delve into his darkest pain and write a book that will help others know step-by-step how to survive and carry on. I did not know Bill Jenkins when he tenaciously tried to get me a copy of *What to Do When the Police Leave*, but when I finally got it and started reading, I knew it was important and crafted of compassion and love at great sacrifice. Mr. Jenkins' book is a magnificent gift. It is for all of us.

Patricia Cornwell
December 2000

I am embarking on a journey of suffering which begin August 12. ... [O]ut of this one tragedy, we have set ourselves a challenge to see just how many good things we can bring.

Internet Newsgroup Post, August 1997

Preface

This book is different from other books on grief and loss in two ways. First, it is a victim's voice reaching out to other victims and survivors of traumatic loss with practical advice born from firsthand experience. I have tried to speak from the inside of grief, not the outside looking in. The advice in this book is the result of countless hours of personal mourning; working with and talking to victim advocates and other professionals; and most importantly of all, talking to other victims and survivors, some very young in their grief, and others with many long years behind them.

Second, it is not a retelling of our story. Instead, it is a guidebook to help you along your way. It is frank and simple advice – information that has been directly helpful to us and others. It is a collection of all the things we could think of that family and friends need to know following a tragic loss.

Every effort has been made to ensure that this information is sensible and responsible and is in accord with prevailing and generally accepted practices. This book is not intended to *replace* professional medical, psychological, legal, or spiritual counseling. Hopefully, it will be an invaluable tool for these caregivers as they help you with the difficult journey ahead.

This book is written solely from the victim's perspective. Experts in various fields made valuable contributions when needed, but grief is as varied and complex as life itself and each individual and situation is different. You must find what works best for you and your family in the days ahead. I hope that this book will help make your first steps along this path healthy ones.

No one ever told me that grief felt so like fear. I am not afraid, but the sensation is like being afraid. The same fluttering in the stomach, the same restlessness, the yawning. I keep on swallowing.

At other times it feels like being mildly drunk, or concussed. There is a sort of invisible blanket between the world and me. I find it hard to take in what anyone says. Or perhaps, hard to want to take it in.

C. S. Lewis
A Grief Observed

We are all in this together; we're all walking hand in hand. Hold on tight and maybe together we can make this ride a little less rocky.

Internet Newsgroup Post, December 1997

"What Do We Do Now?"

If you are reading this book after being notified of the death of a loved one, you are no doubt asking, as many others have, a difficult question: "What do we do now?" Traumatic loss – whether through homicide, car crash, suicide, accident, or any other factor – is a shocking, life-changing tragedy which leads to a roller coaster ride of emotions, events, and feelings.

This book is designed to help pave the way for you in making some of the most important decisions in the days ahead, and to help you understand some of the natural processes which take over when we experience this kind of loss. It is the kind of book that I should have received when first informed of my son's death the night he was shot and killed. He was on his second day of work when the restaurant where he was employed was robbed at closing time by a gunman assisted by two young female accomplices. All are now serving lengthy prison terms for robbery and murder.

If you are like many people, you probably don't feel like reading anything right now, but at least try to get through the next chapter, or give this book to a family member or friend to read for you. Some very valuable advice is contained here – advice which others have paid a dear price to be able to give.

This book would not be possible without the contributions of survivors of traumatic loss – willingly given in order to help survivors of traumatic loss – and the input of the professional caregivers and victim/witness advocates who work with them.

Much of what is contained here comes from firsthand experience, with considerable input from those who work with survivors of traumatic loss on a daily basis. The work of professional therapists, psychologists, and grief counselors, while important to the grief process, is not represented here in great detail. Instead, you will find practical information contributed by people who have been in the same position you are in right now.

At the beginning of this book, you will find a checklist of basic information which will be useful immediately. After that, you will find more detailed information which will be helpful in the near future. There are also chapters on more long-term concerns such as how grief affects us and what to expect from the justice system.

In the back of this book you will find a place to record important phone numbers and lists of helpful organizations and agencies, books, and other resources which may help you. You will also find two pages you may copy to give to your friends.

All throughout this book very frank language is used. Not to seem harsh or insensitive, but the reality of the situation cannot be minimized, sweetened, or postponed. Be aware that in this book you will never see death referred to in softer terms such as "passed away." Death will be met head-on and wrestled with in our attempt to adjust to our lives as they are now, without our loved one with us.

Please note that not all the information presented here may apply in your situation. Feel free to choose whatever seems to be best for you. No one can give an *exact* set of steps for you to follow, and no one can, or should, tell you how to properly grieve. That is up to you and your family to experience for yourselves, and it will be different for everyone depending on the situation, on the personalities involved, and on the amount and kind of support you receive during the process.

Decide what works for you. Offered here is advice from those who have been there before you. We hope it will be helpful to you in the coming days and weeks, and that you will find some measure of peace in your journey.

As long as there are things to do and events to manage, we will continue to be productive. What happens when the busy-ness stops? ... I will not sit in the shadow of death so long that I become a shadow, myself.

Journal Entry, August 1997

The Checklist

There are eight things that you need to immediately consider. These essential guidelines are summarized here and are dealt with in greater detail in the next chapter. Go to the page shown for more information on a specific topic. Later, you may want to read some of the other chapters which will help you understand what to expect further down the road.

1. **First, if you have not done so already, start gathering your support system around you.**
(Page 17)

   - You will need to express strong emotions and talk about what has happened and how you feel. It is not healthy to suppress these natural urges. It is important to have trusted friends and family around who can listen to you and share memories.

   - People will want to help in many ways. Be sure to set some limits on those helping with housecleaning.

2. **Second, have a support member start notifying the people who most need to know.**
(Page 19)

   - Notify those who can most easily contact others for you.

   - People who are frail or may react badly to the news should be notified in person if at all possible.

- Talking to children about the death must be handled especially carefully. If possible, read the chapter on "Children and Grief" before talking to them.

3. **Next, identify those in your support system who will be responsible for protecting your privacy with the media.**
(Page 20)

- You may be approached by reporters. Determine how you will deal with their questions.
- Decide whether you want to watch the news coverage on your case or not.
- You may want to record news coverage for later.

4. **Try to get some rest and start thinking about your health.**
(Page 24)

- Contact your family doctor to talk about your health as soon as possible. Meeting with a grief counselor may be recommended.
- Get time off from work related responsibilities if possible. You will be easily distracted. Be extra careful on the job and while driving.
- Do not try to maintain an appearance of false strength. Be honest with others about your emotions. Nobody expects as much from you as you do right now. Take it easy on yourself.
- Recognize that everyone grieves differently.
- Do not fall into the trap of feeling *guilty* about an event which you could not have affected.
- You will experience physical and emotional effects of grief *beyond your control*. Be prepared for them.
- Get regular exercise, eat well, and get proper rest.
- Be wary of those who may try to take advantage of you. *Never* give out credit card numbers or personal information over the telephone.

5. **Funeral arrangements will need to be made soon.**

(Page 34)

- Religious observances may need to be communicated to the authorities and those handling the body of your loved one as soon as possible.

- Be sensitive to the input of those close to your loved one when making arrangements, but keep the number of decision makers to a minimum.

- Have family members inquire about *bereavement rates* for travel on major carriers. Some form of documentation such as an obituary or death notice may be required to qualify for these rates. In reality, they are rarely significant bargains.

6. **Talk to the police further.**

(Page 35)

- Discuss the case with them cooperatively.

- Treat the information they share with you as confidential so the investigation is not jeopardized.

7. **Other difficult things you may be called upon to do:**

(Page 37)

- Identifying the body will be emotionally difficult. Have someone go with you if you have to do this.

- If you are a witness, police and others may need to question you.

- Make priorities for what is most important right now and don't do less important things.

- You may need to reclaim personal belongings.

- If you relocate, make sure the police know how to contact you. If your home is the crime scene, you may need to contact a *biohazard* cleanup company.

8. **Dealing with other legal matters related to the death:**

(Page 39)

- The funeral director will obtain the death certificate and help you determine how many copies to ask for.
- If a will exists, locate it immediately.
- Begin dealing with the associated costs of the death.
- Begin filing insurance and other related claims.
- Don't make life-changing decisions right away or without consulting with a trusted advisor.
- You may want to consider a memorial gift or request contributions in your loved one's memory.

Each item above is discussed in more detail beginning on the pages given. If you have time, take a look at these now and read some of the later chapters when you have a need for them. You do not need to read this book from cover to cover in one sitting. Take it in bite-size pieces and take your time. Be gentle with yourself that is important right now.

It is time to begin getting to know this new companion called Grief. It will be with you for quite some time. Many people ask, "When will I be the way I was before this happened?" No one can give you an answer to that question right now. You must simply take one day at a time and concentrate on realizing the best possible outcome for yourself using the resources available to you.

These resources are of two types: *internal*, or your personal resources – the ones you bring with you based on what kind of person you are, your beliefs, your strengths and weaknesses, and your personality. And *external*, or your support system – the people around you, support agencies and organizations, your doctor, your family, your friends, your clergy, the books you read, the meetings you attend, and anything else which helps you with this major transition in your life.

You *will* get through this. You will get through the days ahead as all of us have, one day at a time – one hour at a time if need be. You will discover that you have strength that you never knew existed. Don't give up hope in yourself, your support system, or the situation.

It's the one governmental program you don't want to be served by, but when you need it, you're glad it's there.

Magazine Interview, March 1998

Your Local Victim Assistance Program

If your loved one was a victim of a crime, you should soon be contacted by a local victim assistance program, if you have not been already. This agency may become an important part of your life in the coming weeks and months as you begin to deal with the justice system and the grieving process.

In some parts of the country, victim assistance programs are administered by the local prosecutor's office. Elsewhere, they may be administered by police or sheriff's departments, or they may be independent organizations staffed by experienced volunteers. These programs have been created to help victims of crime through the criminal justice process. *Victim advocates* are bound by a code of professional ethics to ensure that crime victims are treated with dignity and respect, that they understand and exercise their rights as victims of crime, that they receive compassionate and fair treatment during their experience with the judicial process so that they are not *revictimized*, and that privacy and confidentiality are protected.

You will find these programs referred to throughout this book. Though the type and scope of victim assistance programs may vary from one locality to another, programs such as these are now in place in nearly all parts of the country. They are the government agencies that no one ever wants to be served by, but when tragedy strikes, their services are invaluable.

As a result of public and private initiatives, many states have passed some form of victim rights legislation. These laws typically define a victim as: (1) a person who has suffered physical, psychological, or economic harm as a direct result of the commission of a felony or violent misdemeanor; (2) a spouse or child of such a person; (3) a parent or legal guardian of a minor victim; (4) a spouse, parent, or guardian of someone who is incapacitated or was the victim of a homicide.

Your loved one is the victim of the crime itself, but because of that death you are a victim as well. As such, you are entitled to certain rights with which your victim assistance advocate will assist you. A copy of the proposed *Victim Rights Amendment to the United States Constitution* is included in the back of this book for your reference. While Congress has not yet passed this legislation, many states already have similar measures in place to ensure that victims will be adequately informed and fairly treated throughout the judicial process. Talk to your local prosecutor's office or victim assistance office to find out how you can take full advantage of the rights and protections afforded to you as the surviving victim of a crime.

The staff of your local victim assistance program will provide you with support, but they will need your cooperation in order to be most effective. They are responsible for helping not only the victims of the crime, but often the witnesses for the prosecution as well. You will find that you will be as helpful to them as they will be to you. Be open and cooperative with your victim advocates. They are there to help you; however, they can only assist you to the extent that you allow them.

What do I do if...?

If I am unsure of the victim resources available?

If you are unsure of what victim assistance resources are available in your area, contact your local prosecutor's office directly, or the *National Organization for Victim Assistance* listed in the Appendix.

If your loss is not considered a "crime," a suicide or fatal accident, for example, a victim/witness assistance advocate may or may not contact you. That should not stop you from contacting that office if you need referral to other local resources to help you and your family in this difficult time. Hospices are also excellent resources for information.

Infants cry until they feel better or can cry no more. I now know this is true for an adult in grief, as well. ... You will get better, although it is more of an adjustment than a cure.

Journal Entry, October 1997

First Things First

T he following items match the headings in the checklist on the previous pages. Some items will refer you to later chapters of this book where you can find more complete information on that topic.

- **First and foremost, if you have not done so already, start gathering your support system around you.**

Call in the key members of your family, friends, and neighbors. These people will be able to help around the house for a few days and will also help provide the emotional support you will need to plan and get through the funeral. That will be your first big hurdle.

More than anything, these people will be there to listen to you and support you. You will probably feel a strong urge to talk about how you feel and what happened. *If you want to talk, even if all you can do is cry, don't suppress it.* It is important for those in grief to be able to talk about their situation and express strong emotions. Sharing your story repeatedly with others is a very important step in coming to grips with this tragedy.

People will want to help in many ways. Helping you helps them begin to deal with their own sense of loss. But often, well-intentioned family and friends try to help by cleaning up for you. They may even have the mistaken idea that removing all reminders of your loss will reduce your distress and be helpful to you. This, of course, should be *your* decision, not theirs. You should firmly set some limits in this area and enforce them.

Some of the things you may want to consider putting off limits for right now are your loved one's room, bed, clothing (dirty and clean), photographs, and specific possessions or things he or she may have recently touched or handled. These are items that family members generally want untouched until they themselves are ready to deal with them.

Once things are washed, cleaned, and put away, the smells disappear. This is something people rarely think about but you may want to have those smells around for some time yet, preferring to let them fade away naturally. You may want to sit and experience them from time to time in the next few days. You may find these lingering smells helpful as you gradually begin to adjust to your loved one's absence.

Make sure your friends and family know that their help is appreciated, but try not to let their good intentions push you along faster than you are able to go right now.

What do I do if...?

If people ask, "What can I do?"

- Child and pet care. Not just for the funeral/viewing time but also in the coming days and weeks when you need to spend some time alone to grieve.

- Meals. Ask those who want to help with meals to spread their help out over the next couple of days and weeks. It will be more useful to you than a lot of food all at once right now.

- Yard work. This will relieve you of some strenuous activity and reduce some of the stress of maintaining your home.

- Referrals. Reliable references for doctors, therapists, funeral homes, etc.

- Driving. Dropping off or picking up family members from airports, funeral homes, and hotels. Have someone drive you to the hospital, Medical Examiner's Office, funeral home, or on errands. *People in traumatic shock should not drive.* You may be a danger to yourself and others.

- Volunteers. Each case has different needs. Find out from investigators if there is a place for willing hands – searching, posting flyers, making phone calls, etc.

- **Second, have a support member start notifying the people who most need to know.**

When possible, notify people who can contact others as you feel necessary – key family members, friends, and neighbors; employers; school administrators; coaches; ministers or clergy; scoutmasters; etc.

For anyone who is frail or who may have a particularly bad reaction to the news, every effort should be made to have someone communicate with them in person. Above all, try to reach the people who should know immediately. These would be the ones who should know *before they see or hear the news on radio, television, or in the newspaper*.

If there are children or siblings of your loved one, think carefully how you will tell them and who will deliver the news. This will be an important moment for them. Children respond to death in different ways than adults and often use adult behavior as an example of how to grieve. Suggestions for talking to children about death can be found later in this book in the chapter entitled "Children and Grief."

What do I do if...?

If I have to tell someone else about a loved one's death?

- Speak to immediate family or very close relatives or friends personally rather than by phone if at all possible. Go with another family member, clergy, or police. Do not go alone.

- Gently and calmly prepare them to receive bad news. Make sure they are sitting down. Have other members of the household present for support. Stay calm but not detached.

- Speak clearly, slowly, and plainly. Use your loved one's name and tell what happened in simple terms. Give as many details as you think are appropriate. Answer questions as well and as plainly as you can. Expect any response.

- If they exhibit medical distress, call the Rescue Squad.

- Never leave anyone alone after telling them of the death of a loved one. Wait for additional support to arrive before leaving. Offer to make some phone calls, if needed.

- **Next, if you have not already done so, identify those in your support system who will be responsible for protecting your privacy with the media.**

Depending on the circumstances surrounding the death, you may be visited by the media shortly. *You are not required to give any reporter any information at all.* The police have media spokespeople. It is their job to give the facts of the case to the media. The reporters can get the story from them.

However, in order to give more substance to their news story, reporters may try to contact you or people who know your loved one. Don't be surprised if reporters call you or a news van pulls up to your door before the day is out.

Your local prosecutors and victim assistance advocates deal with reporters all the time. You should talk to them before you have *any* contact with the media. They should be able to give you very valuable advice on how the local news media conduct themselves and what to expect.

If your case commands national attention, you may find yourself at the center of a real frenzy of activity. Reporters from out of town have sometimes been known to be highly competitive, aggressive, and even intrusive as they gather information. Media coverage of national disasters and tragedies may last for days or even weeks. Reporters may expect or even demand access or interviews, rather than request them. In some recent high profile tragedies, they have even been known to misrepresent themselves in order to get close to victims and families.

Victims and their families quickly find that they do not have the strength or experience to deal with this much attention from so many reporters. It is in these situations where the authorities, relatives, and friends often perform the much needed service of protecting the family from unwanted media attention and intrusion.

Perhaps one day the more aggressive members of the media will stop looking at grief as a way of getting ratings and approach tragedy with more sensitivity and genuine concern.

Until then, victims and their families will have to protect themselves as best as they can. Insulate yourself and your family if you don't want public exposure. Take care of your health and your grief first, that is the most important thing.

Don't let others distract you from what you need to do right now. At the same time however, *don't shut out those that are there to help you.* Take advantage of the trained and caring resources available to you during this time. If you have doubts about someone's identity, ask to see some credentials. Legitimate caregivers or members of a *Crisis Response Team* which has been dispatched to help a community begin to deal with a tragedy will easily be able to identify themselves as such.

You are under no obligation at all to talk to reporters, give interviews, or share information with them. In fact, it is probably best if you have as little contact with the news media as possible right now. Let your family's representative handle direct contact with reporters for the time being. This way, you will still be able to provide input into the story without exposing yourself to too much attention.

If you do decide that you want to release some information, limit it to basic background facts about your loved one. A recent picture (the camera can crop out others in a photo if necessary); general information on your loved one's interests, hobbies, school, job, future plans; memorial funds (if planned); and other specific human interest elements will be plenty.

Keep in mind that sharing this information is entirely your decision and should be well thought out and perhaps written down beforehand. Keep the focus on your loved one and how you want them perceived and remembered by the public.

Do not include comments on the case or the suspects, specific addresses, reactions which may be interpreted as intended legal action, how you feel about a particular social issue such as gun control or the death penalty, and you absolutely *should not* discuss any details of the case or anything the police may have already told you in confidence. Witnesses to the crime should not talk to the news media at all as they could quite possibly jeopardize the case's investigation by doing so.

Knowing even the smallest details following a crime can be helpful to a suspect who is trying to avoid capture or prosecution.

Unfortunately, even if you do not want to talk to them, some contact with the media may be unavoidable. Legally, they can take pictures of you in any public place – entering or leaving a building, courthouse, or even a funeral home, for example. If you find that your emotions are overwhelming, avoid walking past the camera, find another exit, or simply wait until the reporters go away. It is best to avoid confrontations if at all possible – very little will be gained from them.

Through it all, do not let the media interfere with your grief, and do not allow your grief to be presented for public consumption without your consent. It is your choice whether to allow your shock, sorrow, anger, and frustration to be seen by others, not the media's.

Often, those involved in a tragedy such as this will see an enormous amount of media attention immediately. Then, as more pressing matters take over the world, they find that this attention abruptly stops. This is a normal and characteristic way that news coverage is handled in our society as, one by one, new and exciting things grab the attention of a distractible public.

For some, it is a relief that they do not have to see the event recounted on the news. Others may feel forgotten by the community, bringing a sense of abandonment and insult that the event which took their loved one's life should be so quickly forgotten. It is something you should be prepared for.

Depending on how you feel, you may or may not want to watch the news for several days. Some people can't stand to watch the news during this time; some are glued to the television. It is completely up to you as an individual, but there is something you should understand about how things will go for the near future: You will be an *observer*, not a participant in the investigation and the media coverage surrounding it.

There really is very little you can do to control the media coverage. Depending on the situation and circumstances, your case may get sensationalized; contain misquotes, incorrect assumptions, embarrassing or even completely wrong information; or spin wildly out of control. If you have any questions at all regarding your case, *rely on the police for the facts, not the news reports.*

During the first few days of media coverage, and depending on the details of your case, you may want to ask friends to help you videotape the news as it appears so that you will have it available for later review and reference. Of course, you should try to save all the original newspaper stories that appear. If your local television stations and newspapers have Internet websites, you can often retrieve the text of their news stories from there on the same day or week that they are covered.

One final concern needs to be mentioned regarding the media and its treatment of crime victims. Sometimes talk shows will invite victims and/or their family members to appear on television shortly after their victimization. These victims are then at the mercy of the producers and hosts who may or may not have the best interests of the guest at heart.

If, following your loss, you are approached by the producers of a local or national television talk show, seek wise counsel before you decide to participate. You may need to put some distance between you and your loss before you are up to such a task. The National Center for Victims of Crime (address in the Appendix) has developed a "Guests' Bill of Rights" for television talk shows. Contact the NCVC and ask for a copy, or you can read it online at their website.

Whatever happens, be sure to take care of yourself during these next few days. Do not let the media intrude on your private grieving time or let the coverage affect your ability to do what you have to do right now. It is your choice to allow your private grief and anguish to be made public, not theirs. You may welcome the media's involvement if some potential good or community healing will come from it. But throughout the grieving process, you must take care to protect yourself from further victimization. Remember, when it comes to your privacy and the privacy of your family, *YOU* are in charge.

What do I do if…?

If the media ask for an interview?

If the media ask for an interview, you can legitimately:

- Refuse the request, or ask a family member or friend to speak on your behalf.
- Request a specific reporter to do the interview.
- Request that the media respect your family's right to grieve in private and request that they not approach certain family members.
- Control all aspects of the interview such as who is present, when and where it takes place, and how long it will last.
- Refuse to answer any questions that you would rather not answer.
- Insist on protecting your privacy and that of your family. You may request that only first names be used or that aliases be substituted if identities are particularly sensitive.
- Ask to know what approach the reporter will take to the story.
- Expect to be treated with dignity and respect.
- Ask to review questions beforehand, and review quotations before they are published.
- Demand a retraction or correction if the media reports information incorrectly.
- Change your mind about granting interviews.

The *National Center for Victims of Crime* has materials listing rights such as these, and other information helpful when working with the media. These materials are available through their website or by contacting them at the address and phone numbers listed in the Appendix.

● **Try to get some rest and start thinking about your health.**

Take a deep breath. Walk around a bit. Watch the sunrise or the sunset. The world goes on, and so will you. Take what time you can now to rest up a bit. You are probably still in shock.

This condition may last for several days, weeks, or even longer. You may have trouble concentrating, eating, or sleeping.

Shock can make you feel numb. This is normal. Other people often mistake this numbness for strength. The truth is that your numbness will make it possible for you to do some of the things which must be done in the next few days.

After the numbness and shock wear off, you will most likely experience emotional turmoil – wide swings from one emotion to another as your mind tries to take all of this in. Physical side effects such as nausea and headaches may occur. You may have trouble sleeping or have nightmares and bad dreams. It is also common to experience what might only be explained as mystical occurrences or visits from your loved one while you sleep. You may become easily startled, more aware of your own mortality, or begin to fear for the safety of yourself and others. This is normal. We have all gone through it. You are not going crazy, and in time, things will settle down a little.

Here are some suggestions to help you get started in your grieving process and to help you take care of your physical and mental well-being:

> * Many people have found that keeping a journal or creating a scrapbook or memory book during this period helps them work through their thoughts and feelings about the death and preserves important information for later review and reflection. Find a blank notebook and start writing down everything you think and feel.
>
> Take your journal with you everywhere you go and use it as an outlet for your emotions. Many people write about how they react to the events of the day. Many write poetry, even if they have never written poetry before. Some write deeply personal things or things they want to say to their loved one. Some write things they want to share later with others or publish.
>
> Use your journal any way you like. It is your record of your life right now and it will be a valuable connection to this time in the future.

Scrapbooks are somewhat different and can have two functions. A scrapbook of memories can give you and your family an activity that everyone can participate in. Children can draw pictures or write stories about their loved one and their memories. It can be an organized place for photos and mementos from your loved one's life. And it can be a place where adults can collect their own thoughts and feelings. Later, these collected materials can even be used to create a *memorial Internet website* in your loved one's memory, if you like.

Some people will want to include the news articles surrounding the death, some will prefer not to. This will be an individual decision based on what happened and what you want to be reminded of every time you open the album. In short, include everything that you think will be helpful and exclude materials which would be hurtful. More intense materials may be kept safely elsewhere.

There is another, very important function that scrapbooks can serve. *A carefully prepared scrapbook can be a valuable tool for the investigators and prosecutors handling your case.*

To prepare a scrapbook for this purpose, use a slim album; you don't want anything too bulky to carry conveniently. Use clear page protectors to hold *copies* (not originals) of photos, mementos, and other materials which will help those handling your case better understand your loved one's life. The more they can put an active human life behind a face and represent a real person, the more effective their efforts may be in getting witnesses to cooperate and preparing for the trial.

Put all the collected information into an easy to read format or list and be sure to include your loved one's personality traits, habits, activities, things they liked to do with the family, and hobbies. Not only will it prove to be a helpful biography for your prosecutor, but it will also help him or her to make your loved one more real to the judge or jury and represent this person that they have never met with more confidence and assurance.

* This would be a good time to contact your family doctor to discuss the situation and how it may affect your health. Grief can create physical problems and it can make existing ones worse. If you have a current medical condition such as high blood pressure, heart trouble, diabetes, depression, or any other ailment which affects your general health, you definitely want to involve your doctor as soon as possible.

* Your doctor may have some suggestions to help you through the initial effects of your grief and shock. These may include prescribing medication to *temporarily* help you deal with the additional stress of your grief, and referring you to a counselor who specializes in grief therapy to help you remain mentally healthy while you are grieving. *Try to remain open to these suggestions.*

If your doctor prescribes medication to help take the edge off your pain, or suggests that you talk with a grief therapist it *does not* mean that you are going crazy. You have received a major shock. Your life has changed dramatically through the senseless action of another. People who try to go through this without the help of medical care are often fooling themselves into thinking that they are stronger than they really are.

Many people deny that they may need the help of a mental health professional during this very difficult time, but at least be willing to try counseling, either with a grief therapist on an individual basis or in a group setting with others who share a similar loss. A good grief therapist has a wealth of experience and resources to help you along your journey. You may need to try several counselors or groups before you find one with which you are comfortable, and you may very well decide it is not for you. However, you may also find it to be a very important part of your grieving process.

If your doctor does put you on a medication to help you manage for the time being, *do not* attempt to change the dosage or amount yourself. If you feel that it is not working as you expect, talk to your doctor. If you feel that you don't need as much anymore, talk to your doctor. Many of these medications must be increased or decreased *gradually* and only under supervision. If you decide to try an over-the-counter herbal remedy, make sure you inform your doctor of that, as well.

Help your doctor help you by communicating honestly and openly about your physical and emotional state.

* For insurance purposes, make sure that any therapist or counselor you visit initially is a licensed professional. Their official diagnosis will be an important factor in the coverage you receive. Make sure you carefully follow all the procedures required by your medical plan. Also, be sure to keep precise records of all your medical expenses in case you need to file a claim with a *Criminal Injuries Compensation Fund* or write a *victim impact statement* later.

* You may need some time off work. Regrettably, you will probably not be able to take as much time off as you really need to begin to adjust to your life as it is now.

You must remember that your shock and initial grief will affect your judgment and concentration. If you must drive in the next few days, be extra careful and alert. If possible, arrange to have someone go with you on long trips instead of driving alone for extended periods with only your thoughts for company. If you normally work with machinery, heights, or in a job which demands quick thinking and alert response, discuss with your employer a temporary reassignment until you are better able to concentrate and focus.

You will be pulled in two directions – the need to keep your job and the need to work through your grief. Do the best you can and try to keep the lines of communication open. You may find that your employer has options and resources available which can be of help to you.

You may want to share this book, especially the sections on "Grief in the Workplace," and "How to Help a Friend in Grief" with your employer or coworkers. They may feel less helpless and frustrated if you can provide them with some practical resources to help you.

* It is very important that you do not try to maintain a false front throughout these first days. You are hurting. Everyone knows you are hurting. No one will mind if you show it on occasion. Trying to "be strong" will not benefit you or anyone else at this point. In fact, you will most likely be more useful to those around you through your honest weakness than through your false strength.

You are under no obligation to "handle" anything right now. No one expects as much from you right now as you do. Be careful of the standards you set for yourself. Be good to yourself. Be fair to yourself. This is important.

You *will* make it through these trying times if you are honest with yourself and others. Denying the physical and emotional effects of your grief can lead to misunderstandings with family and friends and complicate your health. It can even be disastrous or deadly for someone who works in a risky environment.

Remember, being "strong" does not mean that you show no emotion; it simply means that you have the courage and the patience to put your best effort into working through your grief.

* It is natural to avoid the place where your loved one died, your loved one's room, or other locations you strongly associate with him or her. It is also normal to be just the opposite, spending time in those places, reflecting on memories and even talking to your loved one. Some find that in these special places they feel closer to their loved one than anywhere else. It is completely up to the individual. You must decide what is right for you.

These feelings are generally not permanent, nor harmful. You will most likely find that they will diminish in time, fading naturally into the background of your life.

* You may not feel like eating, or you may have food cravings or begin to eat for comfort. You may want to sleep excessively, or you may have trouble sleeping or have nightmares. You may feel completely numb, or you may feel completely overwhelmed by your emotions. These are all potential physical effects of grief.

You must continue to eat healthy food on a regular schedule – *grief and hunger are a very bad combination.* Too much sleep will sap your strength, not enhance it. And you need to watch out for the empty calories and snacks, especially chocolate and caffeine.

There are many outside forces which will affect you. Your mood may change with the weather, the seasons, or even the phases of the moon. You may be thoroughly overcome with emotion without warning, triggered by something you never would have suspected – a song, a picture, a trip to the store. You will probably be edgier than usual and less tolerant of minor annoyances, and holidays will impose their own special demands on you.

Strong emotions are common to people in grief. Know that they can come along without warning, even years from now, and you will be better prepared to take care of yourself physically and emotionally when you experience them.

* You may find it helpful to set a simple, flexible schedule and try to put some organization into your day. Many people find that it helps to put some structure back into their lives. Start by setting regular bedtimes, mealtimes, exercise times, and personal time for yourself.

This might be difficult at first, but you may find that following a simple and sensible schedule will help you feel more in control of your life and avoid some of the aimless activity and disorientation which often accompanies grief.

* After you talk with your doctor, you may want to start a regular exercise program of walking, jogging, or going to a fitness center. It is very important that you get regular exercise in order to remain healthy.

Your grief will make you feel sluggish and distracted, but going for a walk or to the gym can work wonders for your energy level. It can make you more physically and mentally alert and better able to work through your grief.

* Be wary of those who may try to take advantage of you. What has happened to you and your family is now public knowledge along with a lot of personal information. Con artists can easily obtain enough information from an obituary to run any number of telephone scams against you, such as pretending to be a representative of the funeral home or cemetery calling to check on your account or a payment. Burglars will know exactly when you and your family will be away from home attending services. Psychics and spiritualists are very clever at taking your money and telling you nothing more than what you desperately want to hear.

For your protection, *never give out credit card numbers or other personal information over the phone,* deal only with reputable caregivers and service providers, and consult trusted friends and family before accepting or paying for any services which are offered to you.

Anyone who calls you legitimately offering services or requesting information will be willing to send you written documentation or provide references for you to check. The con artist and unscrupulous salesman's greatest weapon is pressure. Do not let anyone pressure you into doing something you do not want to do.

* In these next few days, and perhaps for a long time to come, you will cry. Do not try to resist this natural and very normal emotional expression. Don't let anyone tell you that you should not. It is an important release and it is physically necessary for you right now. If you resist the

urge, especially if you are a man, your grief may be prolonged, or worse, bring about physical side effects which can affect your long-term health.

After a time you may feel, or someone may tell you, that you should not be crying anymore. You must not limit yourself. Cry as often and as much as you need. *There is no time limit on grief and all grief is not created equal.* You are making the rules up for yourself as you go along. We all do.

There are only two rules that you should definitely start with: 1.) Don't head down a path of self-destruction, and 2.) Don't do anything which will hurt someone else. Both paths would only lead to another tragedy. That is not something that anyone needs right now.

At the beginning of the grief process, our bodies and minds must have time to work through what has happened. This process cannot be avoided. There is a difficult path ahead which you must walk. It is time to take the first steps along it.

Much of what you experience will be beyond your control, but you can make some conscious decisions that will set your general course. Will you turn inward, shutting out the rest of the world in your pain, or will you turn outward, embracing the support offered? Will you expect everyone to help you in your grief, or will you recognize that others may need your help as well? Will you give in to hopelessness in your pain, or will you use it as an opportunity to grow? Will you become bitter, fearful, and resentful with the world, or will you try to have a positive impact on society for the good of all? Will you ride the roller coaster of emotions with your eyes open, or with them tightly shut? These are questions you must answer for yourself. No one else can answer them for you.

Get what rest you can now. The days ahead will seem like a whirlwind of activity and you will be at the center of much of it. For more on the grieving process see the chapter in this book on "Grief and Grieving," or ask your victim assistance office for additional resources on this topic.

What do I do if...?

If my doctor wants me to take anti-depressants?

Professionals in grief counseling disagree on this issue, so you and your doctor must cooperatively decide what will be best for you. Some feel that medication does nothing but delay the natural grieving process. Others feel it can effectively ease overwhelming physical and mental distress and enable someone to function more productively, especially in the early days of grief. Here are some guidelines which you should consider:

- Be sure the doctor has experience prescribing this medication and working with patients in follow-up care. Your family doctor may want to refer you to a specialist for this treatment.

- You should have a complete physical examination and medical history done before taking the prescription.

- Read the product literature and do some research beforehand. Be aware of all the potential side-effects and be alert for them. Ask your doctor to explain anything you do not understand. Be aware of what other drugs will interact adversely with your prescription. Never take more than the prescribed dosage.

- Be careful you do not become dependent on medication. It is a *temporary* treatment for someone who is otherwise mentally healthy, *not* a cure or long-term solution. Medications will not exempt you from the natural grieving process.

- Since several different medications are available, each with different qualities, discuss your options with your doctor. Different people can have different reactions to various drugs and dosages. *Be careful driving or operating machinery until you know how your body will react to your medication.*

- It may take several days or weeks to build up levels in your system for effects to be noticeable; dosages may require fine-tuning; you may have flu-like symptoms or discomfort when you start or stop taking the dosage. Be patient. Keep a diary of how you feel each day so informed decisions can be made.

- Never try to adjust the dosage yourself. When it is time to stop, talk to your doctor about gradually weaning yourself from the medication. It may take some time to clear your system and it is common to experience some withdrawal symptoms along the way.

- **Funeral arrangements will need to be made soon.**

It is a difficult task to arrange a funeral. This task is made even more difficult when the death is sudden, and especially when violence is involved. There is much to do, but the funeral arrangements should not be made in haste. Try to set aside time to consider your decisions carefully. If you do not feel up to the task yourself, ask a close personal friend or a family member to take care of arranging the funeral itself, leaving you to make only the necessary decisions.

The first decision you will need to make is to decide on a funeral home and contact them right away. Also, start thinking about dates and times for the funeral, viewing, or other services you may desire. Don't forget to take travel for out of town family and friends into account. Decisions on burial arrangements, cemeteries, and locations for the services should also be discussed before going to the funeral home, if possible.

If you or your loved one have specific religious observances regarding how the body is prepared for burial or otherwise handled following death, this information should be communicated to the police, Medical Examiner or Coroner, and funeral home as quickly as possible after you are notified.

You may have to make an extra effort to inform people of your wishes if what you desire is not generally common practice. Certainly though, you can expect that the people handling your loved one's body at the scene and afterward will do so with the greatest possible respect and sensitivity.

Sometimes, due to the illegal, traumatic, or perhaps violent way in which death occurs, and in the need to quickly gather and process evidence, procedures must be done which may be disturbing or not in accordance with the family's beliefs.

For example, in deaths involving an illegal act or violence, an autopsy will have to be performed by the Medical Examiner. In some investigations the body may not be able to be released to the family right away. In any case, even though you may legally have little or no input into these matters, try to work with the authorities as much as you can. Talk to your clergy and seek their advice and input. It is important to try to come to a conclusion which is as agreeable and as peaceful as possible for you and your family.

When making the funeral arrangements, try to be sensitive to the input of those who were close to your loved one – children, fiancées, stepparents, birth parents, grandparents, close friends. It is easy to accidentally leave someone's input out of the decision-making process in the rush to make arrangements. But, when it is time to talk to the funeral director, you should keep the number of people at that meeting to a minimum.

The funeral is an important part of the healing process. Refer to the chapter entitled "Funerals and Funeral Homes" for more information on selecting and working with a funeral home and the process involved in planning a funeral on short notice.

- **Talk to the police further.**

You may or may not be visited by the police again to discuss the case. If you do meet with them, it will probably be emotionally difficult. They may or may not have more information for you about the incident. You will probably have many questions.

The best chances of a crime being solved are in the first forty-eight hours after it occurs. Any information you or others may have, no matter how minor it may seem, which will help bring the ones who committed this act to justice will need to be given to the police. They need this in order to do the best job that they possibly can with the investigation. *Remember, do not discuss anything the police tell you with reporters or others who do not need to know.*

It is important that you get the detectives' names and cards in case you need to contact them. There is space inside the back of this book for you to write down this information. Sometimes investigators are difficult to reach, and you should remember that they are often working on several cases at once, not just yours.

Regardless of how you might feel about the police and the criminal justice system, you must now rely on them to help you. This can be especially difficult if you are in a situation where you fear for your safety. If the one responsible is granted bail, or if others in your neighborhood are involved, you may feel that communicating with the police may be a problem or even a danger for you. There are no easy answers when one is being intimidated and further victimized by the threat of violence.

If a situation like this arises, talk to your victim advocates honestly about it. They will have experience and training in these matters and may have some options which will help you get through this with less difficulty. They may be able to help you communicate with the police in an indirect manner, or provide you with support in other helpful ways.

Again, you must make the decisions which are right for you, but give your victim advocates a chance to help you to the best of their ability. More information on what to expect from the justice system can be found later in this book in the chapter entitled "The Police and Criminal Justice System."

What do I do if...?

If the police seem to suspect family members?

It is a sad fact that a large number of violent crimes occur between people who know one another. One of the first things the police will try to do is eliminate family members as suspects. It is in your best interests to assist in this process. Take steps to get you and your family members off the suspect list as quickly as possible and help the police move on to other leads. This will reduce media speculations, as well.

If family and friends volunteer to take a polygraph (lie-detector) test, volunteer to supply fingerprint or DNA samples, and cooperate in interviews, that willingness to work with the investigation will go a long way to resolving this distasteful but necessary process. While you may not be legally required to cooperate to this extent, being unreasonably opposed to it may understandably create suspicion and waste investigative resources eliminating suspects by other means.

- **Other difficult things you may be called upon to do:**

    * You may or may not be called upon to identify the body of your loved one in the morgue or in the hospital. If you are asked to do this, it will be emotionally difficult for you. You should ask someone who can give you support during this experience to provide you with transportation to and from your destination.

    * If you are a witness to the crime, you may be called upon to provide a statement or identify suspects. You may also be questioned by the police, perhaps also by your local prosecutor and your victim assistance office.

    Later, the defense attorney or the defense's investigators may approach you. Make sure you know to whom you are talking. If you have a question about anyone's identity, call your local prosecutor's office or your victim assistance advocate for confirmation. Find out from them what the best course of action is if you are approached by a defense attorney or his or her staff.

    You should be aware that statements you supply now may quite possibly be used later in court. You may be called to testify under oath in upcoming trials regarding this information. Be completely honest. Tell the investigators what you know to be true, not what you think they might want to hear.

    * If there were others who were injured, you may find yourself tending to them as well as making immediate arrangements for funerals, etc. Remember, you cannot do everything and be everywhere.

    Make priorities for what is most important and don't do less important things right now. Schedule enough time for yourself to stay healthy while so much is weighing on your mind.

    Allow others to help you with all the things you have to do, or ask them to do some things for you. Go ahead and tell them what you need. Make a list for them and be specific, or ask someone to coordinate help for you. Let your friends and family help you. Helping you helps them to deal with their own sense of loss as well.

* You may have to reclaim personal belongings. Usually, possessions travel with the body, but you will want to make sure that they are accounted for. Your funeral director should be able to help you with this if you require it. You should have items returned to you as soon as possible so that they are not lost.

You will most likely not have any clothing returned. Contents of the victim's pockets, personal possessions at the time of the incident, and jewelry will be inventoried by the police or Medical Examiner and may be kept as evidence. Be aware that if an item is kept as evidence, it might be quite some time before it can be returned to you.

* It is common to feel vulnerable following a crime, no matter where it occurs, and you may want to stay with family or friends for a time. *If you decide to stay elsewhere, make sure the police investigators, the prosecutor's office, and your victim assistance office know how to contact you.*

If you do decide to go away for any length of time, and especially while you are at the funeral home or attending services during published hours, have someone housesit for you or ask a neighbor to keep an eye on things. Burglars read the funeral notices, too. They will know when you are likely to be out of your house attending services. You will have to take steps to protect yourself from people who see your loss only as an opportunity to take advantage of you.

If the crime took place in your home, cleanup services may be necessary. *Do not jeopardize your health by trying to clean up blood or body fluids yourself.* Whether for your home or car, a specialized cleaning company should be contacted to disinfect and sanitize the area and dispose of hazardous biological materials properly. These costs are almost always eligible for payment from a Criminal Injuries Compensation Fund or your insurance company.

See the next section in this chapter on "Emergency Response and Crime Scene Cleanup" for more detailed information on this very important topic.

• **Dealing with other legal matters related to the death:**

There are a number of things related to your loved one's death which will have to be dealt with in the near future. Consider them carefully:

* The funeral home will provide you with as many copies of the death certificate as you will need. You will need one for each insurance company, Social Security, Worker's Compensation, or criminal injuries claim you intend to file. You should keep at least two for your own records. You must have one for each bank and financial institution you may need to contact regarding your loved one's assets and bank accounts. For a wage earner with typical assets you may need as many as ten to twelve.

You should know that the Medical Examiner can delay signing the death certificate until all the tests are done and the actual cause of death is identified. This can take some time. If this is the case, your funeral home director or your clergy may be able to offer some advice on how best to proceed.

* If your loved one had a will, you will need to locate it right away and contact your lawyer in order to have it executed. If your loved one did not have a will, you will need to contact a probate lawyer instead. States have very strict laws about how property passes from one person to another in the absence of a will. It is nearly always a complicated process.

It is important to do this *as soon as possible* as your loved one's estate may be vulnerable to a civil suit or other legal action. Someone may try to sue to collect for damages either for this or a prior, unrelated event if they think that they may benefit from this tragedy.

∗ You will have to begin dealing with the costs associated with the death. It is additionally tragic that following a loss, financial reality sets in and services have to be paid for, medical bills come due, and actual costs related to the death become obvious.

If your loved one was a victim of a crime, you may be eligible for a benefit from a Criminal Injuries Compensation Fund. If one is available in your area, your victim assistance program can help you with this claim. Typically, it is a fund which can help pay for medical and funeral arrangements not covered by other sources.

The Mothers Against Drunk Driving organization has an exceptional pamphlet on dealing with the financial burden following a sudden death. Even though your case may not involve a drunk driving crash, this book is a superb resource and is available from MADD (address in the Appendix) or perhaps through your victim assistance program. Request the MADD publication, <u>Financial Recovery After a Drunk Driving Crash</u> or read it online at their website, *www.madd.org.*

∗ You will need to file insurance claims. Locate the policies you need and contact the agents to find out what steps to take to initiate a claim. Read these policies carefully prior to filing a claim to make sure you are taking advantage of *all* the benefits to which you are entitled. Make sure you locate all existing policies.

Double check with the personnel office of your loved one's employer as well for additional employee benefits which may be available for a death such as this.

∗ If your loved one was killed at work, you may be eligible for a Worker's Compensation claim. Check with the employer involved to find out more about this benefit. If your loved one was a wage earner, you should contact the Social Security office soon. Your loved one's employer should be able to help you with this as well. If your loved one was a veteran, contact the Veteran's Administration for information on benefits, as well.

* There are other legal details you must attend to in the near future besides contacting an attorney to process the estate. Your funeral director may have some materials which can help you with local contacts and here are some general things to remember:

Notify all your insurance companies and benefits plans either to file claims or have their records changed appropriately.

Notify the proper governmental agencies to change the records for real estate, vehicles, voter registration, and driver's licenses. Contact the Internal Revenue Service to find out how to file next year's tax forms.

Inform financial institutions, banks, stockbrokers, retirement funds, and credit card companies of the death of your loved one and deal with each account appropriately. Note that funds held solely by your loved one, not jointly with another, must become part of the estate. Likewise, a safety deposit box will be sealed until an attorney or the executor can inventory it.

* Remember, you are still dealing with the effects of your grief; do not try to do too much at once. Your pain may affect your judgment and you may feel as if you are in a fog. Because of this, *it is advisable to avoid making any major financial or legal decisions without a trusted friend or family member at your side.* It is generally agreed that you should delay any major life-changing decisions for at least one year.

One thing does bear emphasis here, though. If you are approached by an attorney or an insurance agent regarding any sort of liability settlement offer concerning the death of your loved one, *do not sign or agree to anything without seeking legal advice.* Consult the MADD publication,

<u>Financial Recovery After a Drunk Driving Crash</u> for more valuable guidance and advice on this and other financial and liability issues.

* If you would like to have donations made in your loved one's name to an organization or charity, make sure you have that information available for the obituary when you visit the funeral home to make the arrangements.

If you would like to set up a scholarship fund in your loved one's memory, you should know that unless you intend to fund the bulk of it yourself, or unless you or your loved one are particularly well-known in the community, the results of your efforts may be marginal.

A typical funding level for an ongoing endowed scholarship is $10,000. At that level, the fund becomes self-sustaining and allows for an award of approximately $500 per year. Although it is a wonderful way to keep your loved one's memory alive, you may have to spend a lot of energy raising the money for its endowment.

If you decide that a scholarship or memorial fund has potential, a banker or investment counselor may be able to give you information on a philanthropic foundation in your area to manage the funds. Or, you may contact a specific school, church, or institution where the scholarship will be used. They will be able to administer the funds under their nonprofit status enabling all contributions to be tax-deductible.

Once the fund has a home, the next step is to find as much publicity for it as possible. The media may be helpful for this, but only so long as it is newsworthy. Word of mouth to family, coworkers, and friends will also be an important way of letting people know about the fund. The more awareness you can raise, the better your fundraising efforts will be.

Again, don't expect miracles, people will give as they are able. If the fund falls short of your goals, consider making it a memorial gift instead.

All of these details may seem overwhelming right now and financial and business matters often tend to take low priority in the wake of tragedy. Sometimes service providers and creditors will try to accommodate you, but you will find that there is a limit to their patience. Do your best to tie up all the loose ends, or have family or friends help you. Don't neglect your day to day financial obligations, either. It is important and will help avoid future stress and legal problems.

Emergency Response and Crime Scene Cleanup

When an emergency is called in, a cascade of events and responses are set into motion. Often, the first on the scene are the police. Next may be an ambulance crew with fire personnel following for assistance. Depending on the nature of the incident, others may be called – the Medical Examiner in the case of a fatality, crime scene technicians to gather and document evidence, police investigators, additional police officers to keep unauthorized people out of the area. The scene can quickly become a sea of organized chaos as precious evidence is collected, photographs are taken, and interviews begun with witnesses.

Evidence collection is one of the highest priorities of the investigative team and the process can continue for some time. When they are done, an enormous amount of cleaning up may be necessary to restore order after everyone leaves. When violence takes place in our homes the results, besides being an awful reminder of what happened, can create an unhealthy environment to live in. The property and exposed surfaces in or near the area of a fatality or violent crime may be contaminated with potentially dangerous biological material.

If this is the case, it is important to clean up the crime scene as quickly as possible for both psychological and health reasons. For the same reasons, *it is important that the family of the victim or the resident not have to do this cleaning themselves.*

Besides the additional trauma it can cause, there are important health and safety reasons why you should not clean up a trauma scene yourself. Blood and other body fluids can be infectious. Certain diseases can be easily transferred to someone who is not wearing proper protective clothing and equipment.

Residue from law enforcement procedures such as dusting for fingerprints pose no difficulty other than that they are stubborn to remove, but the aftermath of a violent crime or death can create a *biohazard*. The area and its contents must be cleaned and disinfected by qualified and trained personnel and the biological material must be disposed of as medical waste. *Even the body fluids of a close and trusted relative should not be considered safe to clean up yourself.*

Generally, hard, smooth, shiny surfaces like tile and metal are the easiest to clean.   Untreated fabrics and upholstered furniture are the most difficult.   Each exposed surface of the room and its contents must be carefully and properly sanitized before it can be considered safe for you to enter again.

This is not as difficult as it sounds, for the right companies. Reputable specialized bio-recovery service companies have arisen in recent years to handle just this type of hazardous situation. These companies provide more than simple cleaning services. They employ people with backgrounds in public safety – former paramedics, fire and rescue personnel, and police. They have mobile facilities capable of handling a wide variety of hazardous situations. And they will handle cleaning, sanitizing, and disinfecting affected surfaces as well as removing and properly disposing of all waste products and damaged property, including large pieces of furniture if necessary.

The crime scene surrounding a violent death can quickly become a disaster area.   The Medical Examiner and police investigators are focused on gathering evidence and quickly moving on to the next phase of the investigation. They typically leave the cleanup for others.   In all the activity, it is not uncommon for there to be confusion about who is responsible for cleaning up afterwards.

Your victim assistance program or the investigators may offer to contact a cleanup company for you, or they may be able to give you contact information for qualified local companies. If not, you can call the *American Bio-Recovery Association's 24-*

hour hotline toll-free at 888-979-2272. This organization can connect you with a network of certified independent bio-recovery companies covering the entire United States and parts of Canada. Even in rural areas, there is generally a company which can respond in a matter of hours after they have been dispatched.

There may be some dispute about whether an act such as suicide or an accidental death is a "crime." This is an important distinction, for if the incident is a crime you may be eligible for financial assistance from a Criminal Injuries Compensation Fund. This fund, to which your victim advocate should be able to help you apply, may help pay for some or all of your cleanup costs.

If the incident is not technically considered a crime, you may or may not be eligible for financial assistance of this type. It will depend on how the program is administered in your locality.

Regardless, you will need to check with your insurance company (homeowner's for your home, or automobile if your vehicle is affected), to see if they will cover the work. It is a good idea to do this immediately as they may prefer that you use a specific company. If you are renting, you should contact your rental agent or landlord right away. They will most likely have to notify their insurance company.

Generally, you will need to get receipts and keep track of all the expenses as they occur in order to file the necessary claims. Your victim advocate should be able to advise you on how to file a criminal injuries compensation claim and what it will and will not cover.

The cleaning company may have policies regarding what kinds of property they will clean and what they recommend discarding. Generally, the property owner will have the final say, but soft fabric covered furniture should be disposed of. It is the only safe and healthy option. You may need to discuss these choices with the company's representative when he or she arrives.

Once the company arrives to do the work, routine crime scene cleanup can generally be accomplished in a matter of hours. That doesn't mean that there will be no more reminders left of what happened, only that the area will be made safe to return to. Additional repairs to bullet holes or other physical damage may need to be made. Furniture and rugs may need to be replaced. It is likely that you will suffer some personal financial loss because of what has happened. Sadly, many crime victims must bear this burden, as well.

What do I do if...?

If my car or home is the scene of a trauma or investigation?

First, call your insurance company – automobile, home, or renters insurance. Find out if they have specific procedures you must follow. Contact your landlord or property manager if they have not yet been contacted and inform them of the situation.

Do not agree to clean up blood and body fluids yourself. You cannot be required to do so without proper training, equipment, and certain immunizations. Contact a certified bio-recovery company to clean and sanitize the area and its contents if no one else offers to do so.

If the investigators or your insurance companies do not provide you with contact information for services in your area, call the *American Bio-Recovery Association's 24-hour hotline: 1-888-979-2272* for referral to companies near you. Once a company is contacted they often respond immediately in urban areas and within a matter of hours in rural areas.

Keep all receipts for expenses. If necessary, contact your local victim assistance office to see how to go about filing a criminal injuries compensation claim if the incident was the result of a crime. Unfortunately, you may have to bear some of the costs yourself.

If no biohazardous material is left from an investigation, fingerprint powder residue is stubborn but safe to remove with household cleaning solutions.

Tonight I saw friends, family, people I have never seen, people I haven't seen in years. They come for William. They come for the family. They come for themselves.

Journal Entry, August 1997

Funerals and Funeral Homes

One of the great problems of traumatic loss is that it catches us unprepared. No one expects to die suddenly, but whether from sudden illness, evil intent, or accident, it happens.

When sudden loss strikes, wills may be unfinished or nonexistent. No discussion of the loved one's wishes may have taken place. Cemetery arrangements may not be made. Family must travel from out of town on extremely short notice. The costs of the funeral and medical expenses may create unexpected financial hardship. These are just some of the problems which must be faced by those of us left behind.

Traumatic loss presents additional problems which complicate the process of preparing a funeral. Sometimes, several people are killed, resulting in multiple funerals. Young people are killed, requiring special provisions for teens and peers. Violence done to the body or disfigurement may prohibit public or even family viewing. Overwhelming sorrow can make it hard for us to function adequately when making preparations for our loved one. The media may try to cover the viewing, funeral, or burial without permission, intruding on or sensationalizing the grief of the family. And finally, the circumstances, whether factual or rumored, surrounding the death may create social difficulties for the family and friends of the deceased.

Through the next few days, you will have to prepare a funeral on short notice. *Short notice does not mean hurrying your decisions.* Even though it is important to have as few decision makers as possible present when talking to the funeral director, it is equally important to get as much input from as many sources as you can beforehand.

Often, in the rush to make decisions someone is forgotten or overlooked. Those with whom your loved one was romantically involved such as girlfriends, boyfriends, or fiancés may feel left out of the family proceedings or awkwardly in the way. Not being a legal member of the family may leave them in limbo regarding their input and participation, though, depending on the relationship, they may be grieving as deeply as any spouse would.

Sometimes, prior relationships or unresolved family issues can create problems. Extended family relationships can cause strain, as well. Disagreements over decisions and who should make them have been known to turn into ugly and embarrassing struggles for power and authority.

Remember, a funeral is your final duty to your loved one. It is a time for healing wounds, not opening them. It is a time for reconciliation, not resentment. It is a time for everyone to begin working through grief in their own way while supporting others in their loss as well.

Be kind and gentle to one another. Set pride and ego aside, it has no place here. Compromise when necessary, and make this goodbye the best one you can give.

Planning the Funeral

• You should develop some idea of times, dates, and locations for the services before you meet with the funeral director. If your church or place of worship is to be involved, you should contact your clergy as soon as possible to discuss options and scheduling with them before going to the funeral home.

A "funeral service" is generally one in which the body is present. A "memorial service" is generally one in which the body is not present, for whatever reason. The location of these services may depend primarily on how many are expected to attend.

Experience has shown that a public service for an unexpected death can attract many mourners; this is something the family should discuss and consider. Some families welcome this outpouring of sentiment at the funeral. Others prefer a more private and intimate funeral service, followed by a public memorial service planned by close friends and held some days later at a suitable location. Discuss your options and preferences and make a decision with which you are most comfortable.

• Your next step will be to choose a funeral home. You may have one which has been recommended by a trusted source, or with which you already have experience. If you are at a complete loss for a funeral home, you may have to contact several and interview them over the phone, or better yet, visit them in person. When choosing a funeral home, price, reputation, services available, facilities, and location should all be considered.

If you ask for a price list, the funeral home *is required by law* to provide you with one. You should know that the only service you may not decline is that of Professional Services. This category typically includes the normal administrative and business expenses of the funeral home in providing their basic services. Your funeral home director can provide you with details of these if you have any questions. Prices for various additional services and options should be clearly itemized so that you can make an informed decision about the overall cost.

• Once you have decided on a funeral home, set up an appointment to meet with the funeral director as soon as possible. This is where you will discuss the details and arrangements for the services and the funeral home's responsibilities. It is advisable to keep the number of decision makers at this meeting to a minimum. Too many people trying to make decisions or provide input at once creates a great deal of stress.

At your interview with the funeral director you should be prepared for the following:

* You should be prepared to discuss financial arrangements and how payment will be made for the services the funeral home will provide.

* You will need to decide on burial or cremation.

* You will need to provide information on what types of services you would like, elaborate or simple, religious or nonreligious, and where you would like them held – a place of worship, at the funeral home, or elsewhere.

* Be prepared to provide the vital statistics of the deceased. These will be needed for the death certificate as well as the obituary. Education level, Social Security Number, and mother's maiden name may be required to process the proper forms.

The funeral home typically handles composing and releasing the obituary to the newspapers. Be prepared with any additional information you may want included in the obituary. This includes information on memorial gifts, membership in organizations, schools attended, occupation, significant contributions to the community, and surviving relatives. If you wish to have a photo included in the obituary, bring it with you.

* You may be shown into a room to select a casket for burial. This decision can be emotionally difficult. Take your time. If possible, have someone there you can talk with about your choices. For cremation, you may wish to select an urn for the cremated remains at this time or wait until later. You *should not* be expected or pressured to purchase a casket for cremation or embalm if there is no viewing. It is generally not required by law.

• Ask about the condition of the body. When will it arrive from the Coroner's or Medical Examiner's office? When will you need to provide clothing? Will you need to provide a recent photograph of your loved one for the preparation?

Is the condition of the body such that an open casket viewing will be possible if it is desired? If a closed casket is the only option, will you and your family be able to spend some private time with the body to say final good-byes?

Experts in traumatic grief observe that it can be an important part of the grieving process for parents, adults, and even teens and children in the immediate family or circle of friends to spend some time with the body, even in cases of extreme physical damage.

This is obviously not a decision you should enter into lightly, but neither should you decide what is right for another in order to "protect them." Often, not being able to observe the finality of the death leads to regrets and even emotional and psychological problems later. Though none of us likes to experience pain, avoiding it is sometimes not the best direction to take. Sometimes we must endure it in order to release our grief.

Even though it may be a difficult decision, especially for a young person, the decision should be left up to them as much as possible. Perhaps you can ask the advice of a grief counselor and your funeral director before you and your family decide on a course of action. They may have suggestions regarding how such a viewing could be carefully and tastefully arranged.

• The funeral director will give you an itemized list of charges for the services the funeral home is prepared to provide. This will serve to help you estimate the costs of the funeral. Be sure to discuss any charges you have questions about.

The funeral home is generally responsible for, among other things, transporting the body to the funeral home and elsewhere, preparation and embalming, staffing the services, composing and releasing the obituary, making sure that the death certificate is filed correctly and copies are transmitted to you, administrative and ceremonial arrangements, and courtesy referral to other service providers as needed such as florists.

Even though there may be a base cost for the services provided, funeral and related costs can vary widely depending on how elaborate the service is, cemetery costs and care, grave markers and stones, distance to transport your loved one, type of casket and vault chosen, and so on. *Keep track of absolutely every expense related to the death in case you file a criminal injuries claim or write a victim impact statement later.*

If you have financial problems with making arrangements for the funeral, you should discuss your options with the funeral director honestly. They may have some options available that may help. You may also be eligible for help with nonreimbursed funeral and medical expenses through a Criminal Injuries Compensation Fund. Your victim assistance advocate can help you with this.

• If the funeral is for a teenager, many friends and peers may attend. You will most likely find that teens are remarkably good at comforting each other, but they may prefer to be out of sight of the adults. If you can, request a side room off from the main viewing area where teens can come and go, as they like. Place some special mementos there with which they can interact. Try to spend some time with them as you can in order to make them feel that their grief is important too. Spending time with them will most likely bring some comfort to you as well.

• Many funeral homes have "After Care Programs." They may sponsor support groups which meet regularly, hold special holiday remembrance programs, or provide a videotape and book resource library. Ask your funeral director about these resources, as well as information on other concerns such as legal and financial business which should be handled after the funeral.

• The funeral home will most likely maintain your guest book and give you the cards from the flowers. Personalized "Thank You" stationary may also be part of the funeral package. Cards should be sent shortly (usually within two weeks) after the funeral for expressions of sympathy such as flowers, meals, pall bearers, clergy, etc. They are generally not expected for everyone who sends sympathy cards or attends the viewing or funeral.

If, after the funeral, you find that you do not have the strength to send acknowledgements, it is perfectly acceptable to ask another family member to help you, or even take over the job completely. Remember, allowing others to help you helps them.

- Record the funeral for later review. While videotaping is usually not appropriate unless done for a very good reason, you should definitely consider making an audio recording of the service. People who miss the funeral may want to listen to it and even some of those who attend may want to listen again at a later date as much will slip by them during the service. Remember, however, a funeral is an event to be experienced *once*. It can be unhealthy to become too attached to a recording of the service.

For someone who has died suddenly, in good health, and with so much life left, still photographs of your loved one discretely taken by someone in the family or a close friend should also be considered. This is best done before or after public viewing times or before the funeral begins, *not* during the service. Photographs of the flowers are definitely in order. Carefully taken photographs of your loved one prepared for burial can be very helpful weeks and months later as you deal with your grief.

Think of it this way. Even if you never look at the photos, even if you throw them away later, at least you will not have missed the one opportunity you will have to take them. It is a prudent step to take and may avoid later regrets.

- If you want to do something special, or even out of the ordinary, don't be afraid to ask the funeral director about it – requesting a lock of hair as a keepsake or placing items in the casket, for example. It is important that you begin to deal with your grief as you have the need. There are few hard and fast rules when it comes to a funeral, or the viewing for that matter. Don't be shy about making requests to the funeral director. You may find that your request is not that unusual after all.

Funeral homes pride themselves on making arrangements as easy as possible for the family. Most have highly trained staff members who are compassionate, caring, and honorable. Their experience is invaluable as they carefully walk you through the process, trying to make this as gentle as possible for you.

Even so, even if you have no previous experience with planning a funeral, you must still be an aware and informed consumer. Offering unnecessary services, using overbearing sales tactics, or taking advantage of a family in grief is considered unethical, and in some cases illegal.

Some of a funeral home's services are mandated by law, others are individual policies. If you have a question about the way the funeral home is dealing with your family, the services which are offered, or the costs involved, simply call another funeral home and ask if your concerns are valid. You may also contact your state's Board of Funeral Directors and Embalmers if you feel that you have not been given satisfactory answers to your questions.

What do I do if...?

If the funeral is more expensive than I expected?

Typical modest funeral and burial expenses can run anywhere from $5000 to $12,000, not including cemetery and other costs not directly related to the funeral home's services. There are many flexible items that can increase the cost of the funeral, including the number of days of viewing and the facilities necessary to accommodate mourners, the amount of preparation required for the remains, transportation costs, flowers, and choice of casket and other accessories.

Do not feel obligated or pressured to purchase more than you are comfortable with. *Focus on dignity, not expense.* How much you spend on your loved one's funeral is not a reflection of how much you love him or her. It is important to not take on more than you can afford. Also, many people are considering cremation as a realistic alternative to burial today. Talk with your funeral director and family and explore all your options.

Remember, if your loved one was a victim of a crime, you may be eligible to file a Criminal Injuries Compensation Fund claim to help with funeral and other expenses.

Don't be afraid to remember him in loving and positive ways. His face is in the clouds and his smile is in the sunshine. I often see things that bring a sad smile or a tear when they remind me of him. Perhaps the best thing to do with an empty heart is to fill it up with tears.

Letter to a Friend, August 2000

Grief and Grieving

The most important thing to remember about the grieving process is simply this: *No one can tell you how to grieve.* Grief is a normal human response to a disruption in one's life. While deep grief occurs following a traumatic loss, other forms of grief can occur in other situations as well – divorce, injury, physical separation, loss of a job, and so on.

The closer one is to the life-changing event, or the loved one who was killed, the more pronounced the grief can be. As a result you may see, even in your own family, a wide range of emotions and feelings about the loss itself. This is normal and should not be judged or condemned. Remember, many people don't show their feelings the way others do. What you see on the outside may be very different from what others are feeling deep inside.

Everyone is different and everyone has different emotional and physical needs. Grief is a complex process involving the four major components of your life – Physical, Emotional, Intellectual, and Spiritual. It may take a long time to adjust to your life as it is now. Don't let people push you to "get on with your life." Their expectation that "you should be over this by now" is never going to be realistic or on your timetable. They mean well, but they simply do not understand what you are going through.

As you go through the process of grieving and working through your pain of loss, you will begin to look at life from a different perspective and your priorities will begin to change. You may find your habits and routines changing, as well. You will redefine what is "normal" for you in the light of this loss. Many things in your life will take on new meaning now. Some will become more important; some will become less important. Sometimes we make good progress, learning new ways to function in our daily lives. Sometimes we don't make such good progress if we shut down for a while or get emotionally stuck in our grief. This is just the way that grief seems to work. It can be unpredictable and inconsistent. It takes energy and courage to stay focused on what we have to do to make healthy choices.

Unfortunately, while you are trying your best to keep up with the personal demands placed upon you by your grief (what people often call your *griefwork*), you may also be required to deal with the everyday requirements placed on you by your family, friends, and job. You will be pulled in many directions, and through it all, you will have to learn to deal with the constant undercurrent of your grief and sorrow as a daily part of your life.

People in grief are often very surprised at how intense and overwhelming their emotions are, especially in the first few days and weeks. Most people have never experienced this level of emotional intensity before and there are very few things with which it can compare.

We become frustrated and angry, numb and confused. Our emotions are exposed like a raw nerve and our feelings resist our efforts to try to control them. We are fine one day, and the next we are in a raging storm of emotions that toss us about like a boat on the ocean. One day, we want to clean everything in sight; the next, we can hardly get out of bed.

It is important to remember that *there is no Right or Wrong to a feeling*. Strong feelings will become a big part of your life, and you are not a bad person for feeling anger, rage, or even wanting or imagining brutal revenge on the person responsible. In fact, you are completely justified in feeling this way right now. Your mind is simply trying to process the event as best as it can. You have begun the painful and difficult task of working through the overwhelming unfairness of it all. This is part of the healing and adjustment process. We have all gone through it, and you must too, in order to get to the other side of your grief.

The danger in all of this lies in either becoming obsessed with your emotions to an unhealthy degree, or suppressing them completely. Moderated expression of emotions is important. After a while, these emotions will come more and more under control. *We do get better*, and we do begin to adjust to the loss of one so close. Our grief begins to lift, and the pain lessens. But this adjustment does not come easily or quickly, and we never get over it completely.

You may be able to take some comfort in knowing that you will never forget your loved one. He or she will live in your heart and mind always. As the emotional wounds begin to heal, your memories will become very important. You may even find new things to do which will give your life focus and purpose.

As a result of tragedy, many people find the strength to do things they never thought possible. They form support groups; they testify before legislators; they speak to school and community groups; they provide comfort and hope to people in need. Many good things have happened in society because someone who suffered a tragic loss decided to make a difference in memory of their loved one.

Grief is an ongoing process, not a single event. You will have good days and you will have bad. Let the bad days come and go as they will. Birthdays, anniversaries, and holidays will all take on new meaning now. You must learn to deal with these as best as you can. It may help to know that most people find that the actual day itself is usually not as bad as the *anticipation* of the day. Though difficult to bear, these special days enable you and your family to engage in special acts of remembrance.

As you progress further, you may find some people seem to be avoiding you. Know that this is a common reaction. They may not want to impose on your grief; or they may feel uncomfortable or not know what to say around you. You may actually lose some friends from this, but you will also have the opportunity to make new ones.

You may get to know people in your community who have suffered a similar loss. Those who, up to now, have only been acquaintances may come to you with their own stories of tragedy and survival that you may have never heard. People who know what you need when you need it will offer practical help and "just be there" for you.

Assuring your friends and family of the following will help them to be of most help to you. They must listen more than talk, since words and advice intended to be comforting can often sound insensitive and hollow. They don't need to think of something profound to say, nor will they have an answer to the question, "Why?" either. You will want them to share their memories of your loved one as they listen to you share yours. They should not expect you to, nor can you be "strong" all the time. Their greatest help to you can be in the simplest of deeds.

Others who have experienced loss such as this will tell you that life as you once knew it will never be the same. This does not mean that it becomes unlivable or too difficult to do daily tasks. But it will be different than it has been, and you will need to have the courage and patience to adjust to these changes as best as you can.

What do I do if...?

If my friends are insensitive to how I feel?

There are many reasons why friends may become distant, especially after a traumatic loss. As unreasonable as it sounds, sometimes people behave as if our loss is contagious.

Sometimes, in an effort to convince themselves that this could never happen to them, people around us try to blame the victim, or even the family, trying desperately and unkindly to find a reason why they may be spared our fate.

If your friends say insensitive things, perhaps it is best, in the name of friendship, to try to gently educate them. If they just drift away and lose contact with you, there are many places you can go for sincere, sympathetic, understanding friendships.

Connect with a local support group, if you can. You may make valuable new friends there. Finding people who share a similar loss can often make a big difference in our lives. Find people to spend time with. It is important that you do not isolate yourself from social contact, it can lead to serious depression and other complications.

Men and Women in Grief

You will most likely find that men and women grieve differently according to their own natures and personalities, and according to cultural expectations. If you recognize that these differences can exist, and not be judgmental about how others *appear* to be dealing with their grief, you may avoid misunderstandings within your family and among your friends.

For many generations men have been expected to be "strong," to show little or no emotion, and to be protectors. This can place an enormous burden on a victim's father, husband, son, or brother. Under less traumatic circumstances, a man may very well be able to control his outward show of emotion. But, with a traumatic loss the emotions can be so overwhelming as to create a no-win situation. Try to understand that a man may feel personally and socially inadequate, as well as having to bear the burden of an overwhelming sense of loss.

A woman, on the other hand, can be more freely emotional, both physically and socially. Overwhelming emotions for her may involve extended periods of crying and remorse. She may want to talk a great deal about the loss; while he may become more quiet, or withdrawn. She may want to be more active in organizations and groups; while he may want to be alone, get back to a structured routine, or immerse himself in work or activity. She may want to visit the cemetery regularly; while he can't bear to go, or he may visit alone and without her knowledge. She may need some time to reflect or ponder these events; while he may desire the old familiarity and comfort of intimacy or physical contact.

In this way then, you may see a woman trying to deal with her grief through remembering, while a man may try to deal with his through distraction, or even trying to forget things which are too painful to remember. If he is uncomfortable with extreme emotions, he may try to suppress that which defies domination, never really daring to get too close to the painful memories for fear of what will happen if he were to lose control. If his emotions do break through during a particularly stressful moment, he may redouble his efforts to ensure it doesn't happen again. This is an effort which can be physically and emotionally exhausting, can lead to resentment among family members, and it can be extremely unhealthy if it continues for a long time.

Typically, it takes much longer to work through grief when emotions are avoided than when they are confronted openly. Both women and men may need permission and opportunity to grieve openly in a safe, nonjudgmental environment in order to come to grips with the loss and its effects.

Neither way of grieving is either right or wrong, just different. Each person must chart an individual course through the waters of grief. Try to help and support one another honestly and with as much communication as possible. Maintaining an image is a worthless exercise. *Those rules no longer apply.*

For couples, the stress of grief can place enormous pressure or added strain on the relationship. It is widely believed that a majority of marriages fail because of intense grief, especially after the loss of a child, but research has shown this is simply not true. As difficult as this time may be for you, *you should not assume from the outset that your relationship will break up.*

Many marriages actually become much stronger after being tempered by tragedy. Look to the long term. Get good support from family, friends, and groups designed to help you. Talk honestly about what you expect from each other, and how you can be of most help to each other. Try to work together to survive this tragedy through *mutual understanding*, rather than allowing grief to pull you into isolation and hopeless confusion.

One final note of caution. For both men and women trying to cope with tragedy, destructive behaviors may develop. Tobacco, alcohol, or other drug use may begin, or increase. Minor inconveniences may lead to violent outbursts. Tempers may flare out of control in frustration, driving those who are most needed for support further away.

It is important to deal with grief's stress in healthy ways, not destructive ones. If you or someone in your family needs help and support from a local group specializing in addiction, domestic violence, depression, or crisis intervention, *get it.* Grief can be a treacherous road to despair when traveled alone.

Grief "Stages"

Much has been made in popular culture of the "Stages of Grief" – phases through which doctors have observed grieving people progressing. But you are not a doctor observing the grieving, you *are* grieving and your grief will be unique to you and your situation. These "stages" are not necessarily common to everyone in grief, *nor should they be taken as a defined pathway or schedule for you to try to follow.*

As you read books on the subject or talk to different people about your grief, you will find that not everyone agrees on what these "stages" are, how many there are, or on the words they use to describe them. Some sources may even try to give you an average length of time you should expect to spend in each stage. *Don't let these different medical interpretations confuse you.* Take what seems to apply to you and leave the rest. Grief is a complex process. No one will have all the perfect answers. One version of the "stages of grief" is included here to help you understand what is happening to you *if* they occur.

Receiving news of a tragic loss sets into motion a series of physical and emotional responses. It is as if you have been plunged into an ocean of icy water. Your body will go through automatic changes in order to enable you to deal with the trauma.

You will find these emotional responses occurring naturally, and you may go through all of them, some of them, others unique to you, or you may even bounce back and forth between them repeatedly without regard to any order. They may last briefly, or they may go on for a long time. They may occur one at a time, or in combinations with one another.

Professional and popular opinions vary widely, but there are five major descriptive responses which are often identified with the grief of *traumatic loss*: Shock, Disbelief or Denial, Anger, Guilt, and Acknowledgement or Acceptance.

Right now, you are most likely in Shock, and perhaps you are also experiencing some measure of Denial or Disbelief with what has occurred. It may take some time to fully understand and recognize the facts of your situation. Be gentle with yourself.

Don't try to force yourself to move faster than you are able. Don't try to do things right away if you do not have the strength. Your mind and body need this time to begin adjusting to the news of this tragedy. That is enough for right now.

While adjusting to this loss, we often experience an intense yearning for our loved ones – a desire to have them back, with all their faults, even if only for just one brief moment.

You may expect them to call, or walk through the door at any moment. You may experience intense periods of loneliness or sadness at their absence. You may look for them or call them to dinner before you realize what you are doing. You may not want to sort through their belongings or clean up their room right away. You may have flashbacks or strange sensations as you remember to remind yourself of the reality of the situation. While sleeping, you may have nightmares or vivid dreams about your loved one. Feelings of desperate hope can be especially potent if the body has not been found, or if the finality of the death was not fully realized by viewing or certain identification.

Again, *you are not going crazy.* But, you *are* in mourning. Your mind is simply trying to make sense of everything now. Take whatever time you need to adjust to this major change in your life. Openly talk to those supporting you about how you feel. You will know when the time is right to do the things you are not ready to do now. There is no need to rush yourself.

Later, you may enter a period of Anger. You may become angry at the person responsible, angry at yourself for something you did or didn't do, angry at God, angry at people who are trying to help, even angry at your loved one.

Anger can be a natural part of grief, and traumatic loss in particular. Your life is different now because of something someone else did – you had no control over it. You may become very angry at the person you hold responsible. This is a normal human response, but don't let your anger blind you to what is legally and morally right. You cannot let your anger lead to acts of violence or physical attack. You must not dwell on your anger until it consumes you. And you should try to avoid lashing out in undirected anger at the innocent around you.

Anger can last for a long time. Unfortunately, when it seethes and boils inside with no outlet or discussion it may lead to bitterness, hostility, severe depression, or despair. Anger needs to have a safe outlet. It can be released like air from a balloon, either slowly and gradually in a controlled manner, or else through a destructive explosion. You may need to learn how to redirect your angry energy into constructive and positive activities or work it off in energetic exercise or physical exertion.

One day, you may reach a point where you can release your anger and enter a sense of peace, or at least acknowledgment. For now, it is enough to just take one day at a time.

Sometime in your grief, you may start to have feelings of Guilt. Often, the inability to protect your loved one, or the feeling that your loved one died but you survived, can lead to a sense of guilt which is difficult to shake. You may even reach a point where you feel that you don't deserve to get better.

You may experience varying levels of guilt, depending on the situation. It may be that you feel that you did not appreciate your loved one fully. You may feel that you did something which at worst caused the death, or at the least did not prevent it. You may wonder what you did that was so bad that you deserve to be punished this way.

These feelings you may have now will do you little good. The past cannot be reclaimed. Decisions cannot be re-decided. Words and actions cannot be taken back. And the death of a loved one, whether by chance or through the horrible, willful, cruel, and thoughtless or senseless act of another, is not a cosmic punishment for what we have done or not done. Much of our guilt deals with things we could never have influenced at all, or even if we could have, it would not have changed the outcome.

You must remember that you are an individual and so was your loved one. People make their own decisions and must themselves be responsible for the consequences. You could not make their decisions for them. You cannot be responsible for the actions of another person; all you can be responsible for is how you respond to those actions.

Often, people will begin to ask, "What if I had only..." Be careful with these thoughts. If you dwell too much on this, you will very likely find yourself in a trap of the worst kind. Watch out for it. Even if you feel that it is part of your responsibility to care and provide for your loved one, you simply cannot be ever-vigilant twenty-four hours a day. You cannot hold yourself to a standard which is impossible to meet.

If you are experiencing guilt of this sort, talk with a therapist, your clergy, or someone close that you trust. Guilt often turns out to be very irrational once you begin to really think it through. You *do* deserve to get better, and you should not emotionally punish yourself for what happened. What happened is not your fault, and it is not your fault that it is not your fault.

If you accept the fact that strong emotional reactions will come, it is less likely that they will surprise you. Know that they may last for a long time. They may occasionally arise without warning years from now, even after you have found some measure of peace in your grief. They are part of our growth and we cannot suppress them without harming ourselves.

If you suppress emotions over a long period, often they can emerge on their own terms in powerful ways. People who refuse to work through their grief, refuse to allow it to take them where they need to go along their life's journey, often have unresolved issues with which they must deal at a much later date. The best way to avoid this is by working through it now. Allow your grief to take its natural, and often normal, course. Find comfort where you can. Find strength where you are able.

You may find that your emotions will run in cycles. Think of grief as a bottle which is filled up by your emotions. If you cap the bottle, the emotions will build up to the explosion point. But, if you keep the cap off the bottle and pour it out when it gets full, letting your emotions flow freely in private as needed, you will accomplish much in relieving anxiety and working through your grief.

As you grieve, you may find it productive to follow the grieving rituals of your religion. These rituals have often been developed over many generations and can be very helpful in structuring your grief. Your clergy may be able to help you with some ideas. You might also find it useful and healthy to develop your own rituals for remembering your loved one. Many of the books listed in the Bibliography have excellent suggestions for developing your own observances.

It is best to lean into your grief now. It may be at times scary, even terrifying. But you must walk through this valley in order to make it to the other side. In order to do this, you must allow the wounds to heal. You must permit yourself to grow. You must have the courage to walk this difficult path. You must exercise your heart, your mind, and your spirit in order to move into a deeper understanding of life. You must give yourself permission to get better.

A Few Words About Acceptance

As you progress through your grief, you may find yourself one day reaching a point of Acceptance or Acknowledgment. *Accepting a situation doesn't mean liking it or that it is "acceptable,"* it simply means that you recognize its reality in your life and are willing to determine how you will deal with that reality.

Therapists have many words for this final, transforming resolution. But, no matter how you refer to it, it is the hope for the future. It is the hope that somehow, through this heartbreaking experience, we may reach a measure of healing in our agony, maturity in our pain.

It may be hard for you now to even think that one day you will reach this point, and you should not try to force yourself to get there before you are able. Reaching a resolution in your grief will take as long as it needs to come to you, and it will require a great deal of effort and support.

Here are some things you should know right now as you look to the future:

First, you are unique and individual. You must decide what is right for you, and when it is right.

Second, acceptance doesn't mean forgetting; neither does it mean replacing your loved one with someone or something else. Try to find reassurance and peace in knowing that you will never forget your loved one. They will always have a very special place in your heart and mind.

Third, know that it is better to have your painful memories than to feel nothing at all. This is one of the things that shows our humanity – the ability to feel and remember.

Fourth, acceptance doesn't mean that you no longer hold someone responsible for their crime, or that they should not pay the consequences for their actions. It simply means that you recognize that they could never repay the debt that they owe you and you are no longer going to let them influence your feelings or control your life, no matter what happens.

And fifth, acceptance often brings us to a deeper philosophical or religious understanding of life, death, and our relation to the world around us. Successfully working through our grief often enables us to live a fuller and richer life than many who have not experienced tragedy such as this.

You may hear the word "Closure" associated with Acceptance, but people in grief, especially grief due to tragic loss, often consider this term overrated and carelessly used. The reason is that our grief is caused not by the presence of something, but its absence. Nothing can bring back that which we desperately desire for real closure to exist.

Perhaps it is better to think of our grief experience as one of milestones. We will pass each one in turn, but we are in an ongoing process which will last our entire lives. The active and intense grief that you are feeling now will soften as time passes, but some sorrow of your loss will always be with you.

Sometimes we hear the word "closure" after a trial, an arrest, a conviction, or even an execution. But again, reaching a point of legal finality is only another milestone. The justice system, along with the media attention associated with more high profile cases, more often than not reopens old wounds without notice. It is not generally designed with the emotional state or needs of the victims or survivors in mind. Even a severe sentence is only a hollow victory, and appeals and parole hearings may bring even more uncertainty and intrusion into our world, creating additional stress and pain.

Instead of looking for a final door to close on these events, recognize that grief can be a lifelong process. As you continue your life's journey, pass your milestones as you are able. Don't hurry yourself, and work towards reaching a peace in your grief, one step at a time.

Don't expect many people to have the answers you are looking for. After all, the human race has been dealing with the issue of death and loss for thousands of years, and in some ways, we are no closer to a completely satisfying answer than when we started. Each person will come to the conclusions which are right for him or her. Reaching Acceptance is a gradual process. It comes only after much soul-searching, reading, praying and meditating, and talking with others.

Remember, working through your grief is a give and take process. Take as you need from others who will freely give to you, and when you are able, give freely to others in need so that they may begin to have hope. It is a good recipe for progress.

Roadside and Other Memorials

It is important to memorialize our loved ones. It is one of the things that connects us with them in an ongoing relationship. A memorial or monument gives us a significant or even sacred place on which to focus our grief and help the mourning process along. It reminds others that our loved ones were here with us and are remembered. It even commemorates their deeds and the things they accomplished in their lives.

The urge to create monuments is older than the pyramids. These monuments are our way of making our mark on society's memory. They can be as simple as launching a balloon; they can be as elaborate as erecting a statue. They can be practical, such as playgrounds and scholarships. They can be informative, such as Internet websites or books. They can be symbolic, such as a "survivor tree" in a park. They can even be beneficial if small roadside memorials serve to caution other drivers.

There are several organizations of which you will probably become aware in the future as you connect with the network of grieving families. These organizations will enable you to participate in memorial events and programs. You will also become aware of how others are memorialized and, when the time is right, you may decide to erect a memorial of your own to the memory of your loved one.

One type of memorial which deserves particular mention is the Roadside Memorial. Often, after a traffic fatality, family and friends will spontaneously erect a roadside memorial. You have probably seen these – wreaths, markers, or mementos by the side of the road where someone perished. These memorials can range from the small and modest to the very elaborate. From the discretely cautioning to the potentially distracting.

As understandable as they are, and as valuable as they are to the family, roadside memorials can cause some friction between survivors and community leaders. In nearly all cases, if a roadside memorial is erected on a public right-of-way, it is technically illegal and may be removed by local transportation authorities without notice.

Some families are working with state legislators on laws allowing modest roadside memorials of a consistent design for reasonable periods of time. However, most states have no policies or guidelines to go by and enforcement is inconsistent.

Memorials are important in our grief, and recognizing the place where our loved one died is a significant part of the grieving process. Transportation officials generally understand this and are often sensitive to the memorials, within reason. Some localities will be rather tolerant of a roadside memorial if it is kept small and well-maintained; if it is not distracting to other drivers; and if it does not become a long-term, perpetual or permanent roadside fixture.

Being reasonable seems to be the watchword. After all, it would be additionally tragic to cause another family grief by erecting a memorial which could cause an accident if drivers slowed down to look at it. Additionally, contention and public disagreement arising from a controversial memorial can do more harm than good. Debate such as this can tarnish something so personally important and has even been known to escalate into an all out feud. This then consumes a great deal of energy and creates enormous anger and resentment in the community.

If you do erect a roadside memorial, be sensitive to the legality of it. Work to change the law if you have the strength. And remember to be as reasonable with others as you would like to have others be with you.

What do I do if...?

If I want to establish a physical memorial to my loved one?

If you want to develop a public rather than a private memorial, it seems most effective to network with other families and develop it as a group effort. As victims and survivors band together into support groups they have great potential.

Working with a local group will ease some of the burden and you will be able to take advantage of the resources of the other members. Also, if the memorial will honor many people, you may generate more community support and funding. Here are some memorial ideas which have proven successful:

- Get permission to plant a "survivor tree" at a local park, arboretum, or on public property such as by the courthouse.

- Adopt, refurbish, or build a playground.

- Hold an annual holiday remembrance service with a candle lighting, poetry reading, special music, or speakers.

- Erect a statue. Very expensive, but possible if many families have been affected by similar loss.

- Place a special monument in a cemetery or park.

- Sponsor an annual benefit dinner, event, or tournament and use the proceeds to support local victim services.

- Establish a camp program for grieving children or those with special needs.

Be patient. Be persistent. Stay healthy and do not devote more time and energy to this project than you can handle.

Grief in the Workplace

Grief will affect your productivity, there is no getting around that. It will be harder for you to focus, you may be overcome by emotion resulting from an innocent comment or question, you may find yourself having to take breaks occasionally to "get yourself together." You may need to be assigned other duties temporarily which are less stressful or hazardous than the ones you have now.

Grief can exhibit a persistent presence on the job when one has lost a loved one. It can be even more difficult if many of the people in the workplace are affected, as well. Some employers and supervisors are more tolerant than others regarding this disruption in your life. Some companies have established sensible bereavement policies which can be rather flexible, especially if you are willing to use accumulated personal leave when you need some time off.

While the *Family Medical Leave Act of 1993* mandates guidelines for time off to care for sick family members, an employer is under no legal obligation to accommodate an extended period of mourning. Many have, however, recognized that this is an important element in meeting personnel needs and is simply good business sense.

Generally, you should try to help those at work understand that a profound loss can create effects well into a year later. They should expect that you will exhibit visible signs of grief and distress for quite some time. The more they learn about grief and mourning during this time, the better able they will be to help you now, and perhaps others in the future.

For those who work in a supportive environment, the workday routine may actually be beneficial. For those who work in a less than supportive environment, the additional stress associated with the job can complicate the grieving process. Cooperation and communication will be essential, regardless. Showing sincere effort will be appreciated. Being open about bad days and good days will help people realize that your attitude is not personal or work related. Being willing and able to train and help those who may take some of your workload temporarily will smooth relationships.

Occasionally, if your grief is particularly overwhelming, you may need to take full or part days off from work to recover. It is best to try to keep these to a minimum, for obvious reasons. It may also help if you can point to a specific factor which would cause this to be a particularly bad day, an anniversary or a special remembrance, for example. People may be more understanding of your needs if they know there is a reason behind them.

Throughout this difficult time, try to see the situation from your employer's perspective, as well. Try to strike a fair balance between your personal needs and those of your job. Being perceived as taking advantage of the situation will result in more resentment than sympathy, and being unexpectedly unemployed may increase your personal burden considerably.

It is important to communicate with those with whom you work. If you communicate, you are more likely to get the cooperation you need than if you keep them in the dark about how you are doing. If they are fully aware of your needs and circumstances, it may make future requests for needed time off for medical, emotional, or legal reasons more understandable.

On the other hand, trying to conceal your situation can create great hardship and relationship problems. At the very worst, it could result in you losing your job if frustration builds to the breaking point because others do not know what you need.

It is up to you to take the initiative to reveal as much as you think appropriate and give your coworkers a chance to help you. After all, you probably spend more time with them on a regular basis than any other group of people.

As stressful as your job may be up to this point, grief will create additional stress. It is undeniable that some find that they must change responsibilities, supervisors, or even jobs because of this additional burden. If it comes to this, use it as an opportunity to seek out a better overall work environment, if possible. Those who are able to find a less stressful, more supportive position seem to come out better in the long run.

What do I do if...?

If my employer wants to know how to help?

Employers can do many things to make life for the bereaved easier. Here are some of them:

- Understand that grieving can take a long time to work through. Provide support as long as the need is there.

- Don't confuse effects of grief – distraction, anger, withdrawal, sadness – with the employee's attitude about the job.

- Be willing to ask what the employee needs and how to help.

- Grief can be very distracting. Avoid assigning work which could be hazardous or involve long periods alone.

- Make sure coworkers are aware of the situation. Don't be afraid of showing acts of remembrance. They are appropriate.

- Be as patient, flexible, and understanding as you are able.

- The employee will have bad days. Some days he or she will not be able to come to work. Try to communicate effectively and formally work out some mutually satisfactory guidelines.

- Permit the employee to express emotions and pain and allow him or her to take a personal break during the day, if needed.

- The employee may *temporarily* be unable to function as fully as before. Reduce stress and conflict as much as possible and provide as much security and assurance as you are able.

Getting Support

The most important thing which will help you progress through your grief is to get some support from people who share a similar loss. Many victim assistance programs sponsor support groups. If yours does not, they should at least have information on other local support groups that meet regularly.

Two groups deserve special mention. *The Compassionate Friends* is a national organization which has local chapters supporting families which have lost children regardless of age. *The National Organization of Parents of Murdered Children* focuses mainly on violent death and also has local chapters. Both provide support in a small, moderated group format.

Another good source of information is a local hospice. Hospices are listed in the Yellow Pages and are often affiliated with hospitals. They generally work with long-term and terminal illnesses, but they should be able to direct you to support groups, grief therapists, and other reliable resources in your area. Many funeral homes, larger churches, and community centers sponsor grief support groups, as well. Additionally, there is an enormous amount of support available on the Internet with various *websites*, *bulletin boards*, and *chat rooms* to support the grieving. Some of these resources are listed for your convenience in the Appendix.

If you are getting counseling from a mental health professional or your clergy, either may also be able to connect you with someone who shares a similar loss. You may be able to meet with them to discuss your loss and know that you are not alone in your grief.

Talking with someone who has been where you are now can be of enormous benefit to you. And believe it or not, someone who has been working through grief for many years is often helped by sharing it again with someone who will listen.

What do I do if...?

If I am having trouble locating a support group?

Local support groups may address either specific types of loss or general bereavement. They may have experienced moderators or be self-directed by the participants. If you can't find one which matches your loss, your religious perspective, or just simply "feels right," keep trying. In addition to the organizations listed in the Appendix, try:

- Your local newspaper directory of organizational meetings.

- Asking your clergy, victim advocate, or funeral home director.

- Contacting a local hospice for information on local resources.

- Searching the Internet. There are many excellent live, supervised grief support groups here for virtually all types of losses and bereaved people of all ages. Addresses for some of these are in the Appendix, or do your own search.

What You Can Do Now

There are many practical things that you can do right now which may help:

Writing helps. Keeping journals or writing poetry is a good way to process your emotions into words and keep your mind active in healthy ways. Go ahead, write a book if you want. Finding interested publishers and distributors can take a lot of energy and is beyond the resources of most, but you can always publish it yourself for friends and family. One tip: avoid *vanity presses*, publishers who ask for money up front to publish your work. You can do better for less at a good local printer.

Arts and Crafts help. Grief can be remarkably inspirational. Using your talents to create something beautiful and lasting which requires thought and activity is very therapeutic. Perhaps one of your first projects could be to create a scrapbook of memories of your loved one.

Relaxing helps. Don't try so hard to deal with your grief. We frequently find that our most important progress takes place when we are not trying so hard. When we relax and pay less attention to struggling with our grief, we often make the greatest steps toward our destination.

Talking to Others helps. Find someone who will listen more than talk, someone who shares a similar loss, or someone with whom you trust your emotions. Sit with them and share memories, talk, cry, and start to come to grips with your loss.

Exercise helps. Go for a walk; go to the gym; play a hard game of the sport of your choice. Don't exhaust yourself, and don't do something dangerous alone, but get a good workout and release some of your energy in a healthy way.

Remembering helps. Some people wear a ribbon, black for mourning, or purple for victims of violent loss. This is an act of remembrance. So are visiting the cemetery or a special place, lighting candles, placing flowers, creating a memorial of some kind – perhaps planting a tree, or a garden. It is important for us to engage in acts and rituals of remembrance.

Praying helps. Many people have mixed feelings about God after the loss of a loved one. This is perfectly natural, but try not to close spiritual doors at this time of your life. Even if your only prayers right now are rages at God, praying helps.

Stress Management helps. Don't let other, less important things in your life create additional stress. If you need time alone, take it. If you need to do less work at your job, talk to your employer. If you need help around the house, ask for it. Put your support system to work for you to help keep you focused on the task ahead – working through your grief.

As you are working through your pain and grief, try not to let the loss of your loved one kill other things in your life which are important. Just because your loved one died does not mean that your life is over, too.

What do I do if...?

If the holidays are coming up?

During the holidays, gentle remembrances and creating new rituals and traditions are often better than putting the reminders out of sight. Nothing will erase the pain of your loved one's absence, so many of us try to respectfully honor it, instead.

- Tell stories and remember. If you start, others will follow.
- Decorate and light a candle and let it burn all day.
- Make a memorial donation to a charity or good cause.
- Encourage children to remember your loved one. Their memories will be fewer and should be reinforced.
- Make an ornament with your loved one's name on it.
- Visit the gravesite and leave a memento, flowers, or a wreath. Be aware of the cemetery's rules, some can be very rigid. And *never* leave valuable or sentimental items in the cemetery.
- Create a "memory book" to share with others. Have family and friends contribute their memories to it if they wish.

Remember to take care of yourself during the holidays. Don't push yourself too hard and schedule time to rest. You may not have the energy you once had. Try to share some duties and responsibilities with others. *You don't have to do everything.*

Some Physical and Emotional Effects of Grief and Anxiety

This is, of course, not a complete list. Since everyone is an individual you may or may not experience these effects, but it may serve to help you understand the changes your body is going through and how broadly grief and shock can affect you.

Often, these and other symptoms are associated with *Post-Traumatic Stress*. It is advisable to talk to your doctor if effects such as these persist for a long time, or if they make life too difficult for you to do basic tasks.

Nausea or Upset Stomach

Sleep Disturbances

Digestive Disturbances such as Diarrhea or Indigestion

Fear or Panic Attacks

Sighing and Crying

Muscle Weakness

Confusion or Distraction

Sweating or Chills

Headaches

Difficulty Concentrating and Making Decisions

Minor Hallucinations

Slowed Thinking or Speaking

Dizzy Spells

Excessive Activity

Guilt and Anxiety

Nightmares and Disturbing Dreams

Sorrow and Depression

Feeling Vulnerable or Insecure

Emotional Mood Swings

Reliving the Event Over in Your Mind

Lack of Coordination or Clumsiness

Irritability With Minor Annoyances

A General Feeling of Numbness

Anger and Rage

Questioning Priorities and Life Choices

Forgetfulness

Withdrawal From Society

Lethargy or Lack of Energy to do Basic Tasks

Increased Breathing or Heart Rate

Needing to Exert More Control Over Your Environment

Tightness in the Throat or Chest (A Broken Hearted Feeling)

Feeling That Things Are Not Real or a Disconnection with Life

Lack of Appetite

Food Cravings

Wanting Too Much Sleep

It's hard on the children. He certainly was
doing something right for them to have loved him so.
He was their rock and they clung to him. That rock
has washed away. What will they cling to now?

Journal Entry, August 1997

Children and Grief

There are a number of excellent books which can assist you in talking to children about death, but since you may have to do it very soon it will be covered here in some detail. This is a very difficult and delicate subject. As much as we would like to protect our children from the harsh realities of life this is one area where real long-term damage can be done if not handled properly. While talk about death in our society is generally avoided, especially with children, it is now something that you will have to deal with head-on.

While you are talking to them, it is important to remember that *children look to adults for an example.* If they see that adults are terrified of something, then they will tend to be afraid of it as well. If they see that adults are open in communicating their emotions and feelings, then they will tend to be open in expressing theirs. This is vitally important to helping children understand and deal with their grief.

Their questions are quite serious for them. Try to answer without judgment and with as much understanding as you have. Often children will have observations about death which will surprise you in their simplicity and insight. Many times children wind up teaching adults, rather than the other way around.

Do not forget the children. They grieve just as much as adults, but in their own way. Many times children will observe death from a distance, taking it in and learning what is expected of them before they commit to an action. It is normal for children to seem distant or stand at the fringes of all the activity. Remember, they are watching everything. What they see, hear, and experience will go into the development of their feelings and how they treat death in the future.

Children often need to have permission to talk about their feelings. They might not be ready to talk right away. Don't push them into doing something sooner than they feel ready. Later, when they do want to talk, take a walk together; talk in that quiet settling down time just before bed; talk with them if it appears that they may be lost in thought or have some unanswered question on their mind.

Try not to talk to them when *you* think they need to talk. Try not to talk to them when other distractions are around. And try not to limit their tears, feelings, or even their anger. Children often need to express their anger in order to come to grips with it. Once it is out in the open, then it can be talked about and healthy ways of working through it can be discussed.

Children will respond differently to various types of losses. In dealing with the death of a parent, the child may be very afraid of what will happen next. The first question may be "Who will take care of me?" The child needs to feel secure and safe, loved and cared for. There is a need to know that no matter what happens, no one will replace that parent, though it is possible that there will be someone later who will fill that role in his or her life.

Children who have lost a sibling or a friend near in age may feel lonely, guilty, and afraid. Lonely because they have lost someone they played with and perhaps confided in. Guilty for perhaps having once wished that the other child would go away, leave them alone, or even get hurt or die. Now it may seem that this "wish" has been fulfilled. Make sure that children know beyond a doubt that there is no reason to feel at fault for this tragedy, that they cannot cause harm to another simply by wishing it or thinking about it.

Just as a violent death may make you lose trust in society and become fearful for a time, it can have the same effect on children. They may fear for their own safety, wondering if it could happen to them, too. They may avoid crowds, strangers, or even be afraid to go to school. Older children may want to carry, or even sleep with, some form of protection like a pocketknife, a baseball bat, or even a gun. Obviously, a child carrying any item that could be considered a weapon should be handled carefully, especially if they try to take it to school.

It is generally agreed that children must be allowed, even encouraged, to grieve as they are able. Provide them with easily understood facts with as much detail as may be appropriate to their age. Breaking the entire story up into a series of smaller, more manageable talks may be helpful to both of you, as well. No matter what, children will benefit most when you are sincere, patient, and honest with your own feelings and the information you share with them. Children's imaginations are very potent, and lacking accurate details they can very easily create a mental scene which is far more horrible than what actually happened.

When talking to young children, use simple and direct language to explain why your loved one's body stopped working properly. Perhaps they have already experienced the death of a pet or once found a dead bird. You may be able to tie this into your conversation about your loved one's death. Discuss what will happen in the next few days, and ask them to start thinking about whether they would like to participate in some way. You must understand as an adult, however, that a child may react in ways which puzzle you.

Often, children react to death with indifference – not because they don't feel anything or because they don't care, but because they are children and this is how their minds work. It is very important that you do not try to make them feel the way you think they should feel. Just like you, they need to find their own way through their grief. And just like you, their path will be unique.

You may find that some years down the road the child, growing to adulthood, will want to find out more about what happened. This is where the videotapes of the news reports, journals of family members, and newspaper clippings may be especially valuable. Sometimes this experience will even guide these growing young people into very honorable professions in which they can help others who have lost loved ones by virtue of their own loss.

How Children Understand Death

Here are some guidelines to help you prepare to talk to children about death, and which may help you understand how children of different ages comprehend death:

Children under the age of four may sense that something is wrong but will not understand the concept of death or what has happened. Infants may feel a change in their daily routine, in who is taking care of them, or in the mood of their environment. This may cause them to become restless or irritable.

To children this age, someone who was once around is not around anymore. They may react to this in a wide variety of ways. They may show the stress of the separation depending on the relationship, but they will not understand any explanation. Lots of comfort, holding, physical contact, and soothing is in order here.

Children ages four to six may not yet understand the permanence of death. They may not realize that their loved one will not be coming back. They may feel that their own thoughts somehow caused the death, or they may feel abandoned. They may even feel that somehow they are being punished for something they did that was bad.

A simple, honest explanation at a level that children can understand is needed. Do not be afraid to discuss death openly. Remember, for the children involved this is a learning experience and they are relying on the adults to help them.

It is very important not to lie to the child. Do not tell the child that a "long journey" is involved. Do not tell them that your loved one has "gone to sleep." The child must understand that death is permanent. Instead, help them to understand what happened, how it happened, and how they should think of their loved one now that they are no longer present in body.

Children ages seven to twelve are already beginning to understand that death is permanent and that it can strike anyone. They may fear for their own mortality or safety, or they may develop a macabre interest in death itself. If handled in an open and nontraumatic manner, a brief time at the viewing and funeral may be a very positive experience for them, given the proper guidance and attention.

This age range may also feel that there is a punishment involved in losing one they love deeply. Try to help them understand that even good people have bad things happen to them sometimes, and that death is a part of life. It is okay and even natural to grieve, and they do not have to be afraid.

Sometimes children in this age range will "act out" their emotions, create disturbances, or even become violently angry as they try to get attention or rage at events beyond their control. If they have lost a sibling, they may even feel jealous at the attention given to the other child in his or her death. Try to work through these situations with understanding, compassion, love, patience, and a sense of security and hope.

Often, anger in children at this age must be expressed in order to be worked through. Don't expect a child of this age to be able to exert control over these strong emotions effectively the way an adult might. Stifling the anger and emotions of a child can do much more damage than good in a situation such as this.

Adolescents and Teens face a complicated set of emotions when dealing with the loss of a loved one, especially if they were close in age. On one hand, they may desperately need comfort, but they may not want to appear childlike and dependent on adults. On the other hand, they may need to be taught how to grieve in a healthy way from people with more maturity and experience.

Teens are actually very good at comforting each other, when adults are not around to get in the way. If they have a place where they can find retreat in order to support each other, the viewing may be a very important part of their healing. Generally, they will have no difficulty understanding what has happened or its consequences, but they should be encouraged to express their feelings in a healthy way.

Keep an eye out for signs of depression, drug or alcohol use, or self-destructive behavior. Finding a good teen counselor, or an adult friend of the family whom the teen trusts and is willing to talk to may be helpful if unhealthy behaviors develop.

All children may fall into patterns of more immature behavior for a short time until they begin to adjust to the loss. They may also try to behave in a more mature manner than they are capable of if they feel that they, in some way, are expected to fill the shoes of the one who died.

Children should know that they are not expected to "be the man of the house now," or to "be strong for mom," or to grow up to replace an older sibling. These expectations are simply not possible for them to live up to and it is unfair to impose such demands on them. Let them walk their path as they are able, with much love and gentle guidance, and few demands and expectations.

Children should feel that they have a genuine choice about whether to attend the funeral or viewing. If they are not ready to participate, they should not be forced to attend. If they do decide to go, some time beforehand should be spent explaining what to expect. If they decide to attend the viewing, make sure their first experience is as good as it can be – during a private time surrounded by only a very few close friends and family and short enough that their attention span is not strained.

You might invite the child to write a letter to the deceased. Putting on paper, either in words or pictures, all the things they want to say can be very helpful. If done early on, perhaps the letter can be placed in the casket with the body. If done later, perhaps it can be attached to a balloon on a special day and released, or buried next to a special tree.

Be careful of religious terms and concepts that may confuse a child or create resentment. Someone "Going to Heaven," or "Going to be with God," or having been "Taken by God into Heaven," can be very difficult concepts for a child to grasp.

They may feel betrayed if somehow they interpret this as a choice that the loved one made. Bitterness may arise if they blame God for not providing protection for their loved one, or if they confuse "God's Will" with the results of another person's thoughtless or evil act. Needless to say, these concepts can be extremely difficult for adults to come to grips with, as well.

Instead, try to communicate to the child how they should relate to the deceased now. Regardless of your beliefs about what happens when life ends, your loved one *will* live on in your memory and the child's. They can talk to them; they can still share secrets with them; they can imagine them being present whenever they are playing or doing something they enjoyed together. This can be very reassuring and comforting, knowing that their loved one continues to live through their memories and that they have access to them in a different way now.

Children will have lots of questions. Try to answer them as best as you can. If you don't know the answer, tell them. Don't make something up that you think they want to hear. If both of you have the same questions, perhaps both of you can work to try to find some of the answers together.

Finally, children may continue to deal with the death throughout their lives. As they grow, try to give them the resources to process their grief. Access to journals, newspaper clippings, audio tapes of services, and other items will enable them to work through some of the more complex feelings about the death as they grow older.

Grief camps, retreats where bereaved children can interact with each other, have been found to be very effective in helping children deal with grief. A local grief therapist or hospice may be able to help you locate a grief camp in your area or you might try searching the Internet for a suitable program.

Grief and mourning are disruptions in children's lives. As they are adjusting, you may find that schoolwork or attendance will suffer. They may show physical signs of grief. There may be emotions which they have trouble expressing. They may withdraw from the family or society for a time as they try to figure things out. They may need more nurturing or comfort.

They may show signs of being fearful of their safety. They may exhibit behaviors that concern you or try your patience.

Many parents will question a child's progress if emotions are not being expressed openly or if the child chooses not to talk about the loss. Often, however, children try to protect others from pain and distress in situations like these. They may be reluctant to participate in remembrance programs or share their memories, thoughts, or emotions with you or other family members because they think it will make you sad, as well. This is normal and as time passes they may later feel more secure and comfortable about discussing their feelings.

In all cases, try to keep the lines of communication open with the child and with others. Talk to the child's school counselors and teachers so that they know what is going on, and make the child's doctor or pediatrician aware of the situation. Often these people can work with you and offer options that you would not otherwise know about or think of. You are not alone in trying to help the child understand what is going on.

Children are often better able to adjust to change than adults give them credit for. Try to be patient, caring, and give them a sense of security. Don't be troubled if they appear to show no emotion. They are dealing with the loss the best way they know how, by being children.

If children begin to show severe signs of distress, depression, or anxiety; or if various behaviors go on for a prolonged period or become alarming, contact your pediatrician or family doctor for advice or referral to a good children's therapist. Talking to an adult outside the family may be necessary to help children work through their grief. They often see this person as someone who knows nothing about what happened, and as a result they are more willing to talk openly. Good therapists have a variety of strategies and techniques that can help children deal with grief.

Children can and do grieve deeply. They grieve in their own ways, and sometimes beyond adult understanding. Consult some of the resources listed in the Appendix for more information on talking to children about grief.

What do I do if…?

If teachers and school officials ask how to help a child?

The school is in a unique position to support a grieving child. It is the child's daily focus, social center, and where the child is regularly exposed to influences and people from outside the immediate family. Very strong relationships exist here.

Naturally, when children mourn we expect that schoolwork may suffer, they may be distracted and unfocused, and they may even act-out disruptive behaviors. Their life has taken a difficult turn. They don't know what they need and they are in a place where structure may leave little room for personal grieving. Feelings of isolation and "being different" can quickly set in.

School can be a very supportive place. If those at school are good listeners, sympathetic to the child's needs, and honest and available, much can be accomplished.

Adults at the school may want to keep the following in mind:

- Help the child integrate grief into his or her life and activities. Try not to discourage this, *especially* in art or other individual creative projects. The child cannot leave grief at home.

- Encourage other students to be sympathetic and supportive.

- What a child needs most is someone to talk to and listen to them without judgment. The bond between teacher and student may be valuable in fostering trusting communication.

- Don't be afraid to teach about death and grief. It is a life event for which we are rarely well enough prepared.

- Take advantage of all the resources available – counselors, school psychologists, grief literature and books for children.

- Don't be afraid as an adult role model to show your own emotions. Children model their behavior on that of adults. Suppressing strong emotions can lead to serious effects later. Allow and even encourage the expression of emotions in the proper settings. Give the child permission to seek refuge in a safe, quiet environment whenever they feel overwhelmed.

- If serious disruptive behaviors or other acts which cause concern emerge, refer the child and family to professional bereavement resources. Discipline alone can hardly resolve the root cause, especially if the child adopts an "I don't care" attitude. How the child works *and* plays will be very telling.

Love Song

And the river is wide
And the ocean is deep
And although I have tried
I cannot fall asleep

And the prairie is wide
And the forest is deep
And although I have cried
I will no longer weep

And the heavens are full
And the moon on your cheek
And in this endless lull
I no longer feel weak

I will be here for as long as I can
I will live year to year holding your hand
I will fill every wish where you stand
I will be love for you, simple and grand

And this city I know
And this home is so dear
And although I must go
I will always be here

And the heavens are full
And the starshine is bright
And in this quiet lull
How I love you tonight

Susan Greenbaum
In memory of her brother Ronnie
Available on the album,
Wake Up!, Planetary Records

Tough day today. One month after. Trying to think of something profound to write on a day that should be significant. Can't thing of anything. That in itself is probably profound enough.

Journal Entry, September 1997

Grief Responses

There are different types of grief responses that arise when we are confronted with different types of death. People grieving a loss resulting from long-term or age-related illness will find that the grief response can be very different when they are notified that their loved one has been killed in a car crash. Someone whose loved one drowned while swimming would react differently if the death resulted from a suicide or murder.

It is obvious that our loved one's age, gender, and relationship to us play a major role in how we respond to the news of a death. But, we may find that it is also colored and shaped by how we are informed, whom we feel is to blame, and how the death occurred. The combination of these elements forms our initial grief response. This response may govern how we think about the death for quite some time. Later, as we continue to deal with the long-term consequences of the death, we may find that this initial reaction changes, mellows, softens, or deepens in some way.

Let's look at how different factors can influence our grief response:

The Notification

It all starts when someone notifies us that our loved one has been killed or is dying. This sets into motion a crisis response in our bodies which can include increased heart rate, increased energy level, and a heightened mental focus as the reality of the situation hits us with full force. As long as there is something that requires our activity – searching for our loved one, getting to the hospital, making decisions about what to do next – our bodies will function on a state of high alert. When the action subsides, exhaustion follows as we are finally able to relax.

If there is nothing to be done, no search to mount, no hospital to visit, no crisis to confront, we can instead become bewildered at the news and its reality may take time to sink in. When we are informed by the police or notification team, we may collapse in tears, accuse them of lying to us, or even become violent. Police officers and other caregivers are trained to expect a wide range of reactions when giving a death notification and law enforcement has long recognized that this is a most unpleasant and difficult responsibility. Regardless of how they appear to you, those with the sad duty of delivering this news often find themselves emotionally drained afterward.

When we receive that first visit, we may suspect or even begin preparing for some sort of bad news when we answer the door, desperately hoping that it will not be the worst. But, when we are gently and firmly informed of what has happened we are shocked and devastated. Our lives are changed forever. Some people remember every word spoken to them in these moments and through the first few days, some remember nothing.

When the notifying officers or team leaves, an eerie calm settles over the room and the sad task ahead begins. Though traumatic, jurisdictions generally try to handle death notifications with some sense of compassion and sensitivity, and this is perhaps the best one can expect at this point.

Unfortunately, many people are exposed to much more traumatic experiences. Depending on the situation, some may receive a call from the police instead of a visit. Being present during the death or fatal injury, receiving a phone call from someone who was trying to be "helpful" or even hurtful, or hearing or seeing a breaking news story can all short-circuit a controlled death notification process. For those who found their loved one's body, or if their loved one had been missing or unreachable for some time; if the body has not been found, or if serious injury or damage has been done, the additional stress and trauma of the experience can have far-reaching and distressing effects on various members of the family and friends.

In situations like this, it is important to take advantage of as much support and help as is available. Talking with someone you trust about what happened and your reactions to it is an important step in working through the memories which result from seeing and hearing things which no one should ever be exposed to.

Memories created during times of crisis are by nature especially vivid. Later, they can be quite overwhelming, unpredictable, and intrusive. Though it may be some time before they begin to fade, when unwelcome mental images intrude on daily life many people find success in using these unpleasant and perhaps even violent scenes as a springboard to think about more pleasant memories of their loved one.

By redirecting their thoughts from the relatively few but intrusive memories of their loved one's death towards the many beautiful memories of their loved one's life, a measure of peace is obtained. With a little practice or guidance from a grief therapist this may be a helpful technique for you, as well.

Placing Blame

It is difficult, if not impossible, to examine the complex series of events leading up to a death and come up with completely satisfying answers. As we try to make some sense of this tragedy, we engage in an investigation of our own, of sorts. Decisions are questioned and second-guessed, accountability is evaluated, and sadly distressing coincidences are discovered.

Looking at the death and reviewing it in an objective and detached manner can be an important part of beginning to accept and understand the event, how it happened, and what effect it will have on your life and the lives of others. It is natural to spend time thinking about what happened, but as you look at the events and the part each person played in them, try to be fair. Punishing someone or holding them responsible because you feel that they could have or should have done something differently can have a brutal impact on them. Undeserved blame can have a devastating effect on the people involved and relationships with them.

From the time we are children we are faced with two very different but related concepts – placing blame, and accepting responsibility. Children are punished if they are caught doing something wrong. The natural tendency then is to develop ways of avoiding punishment; either by taking greater care to not be caught, or finding someone else to conveniently condemn. Anyone with siblings will recognize this simple tactic.

This pattern continues into adulthood as those who are caught doing wrong try to justify everything from exceeding the speed limit to committing murder. If they cannot excuse their actions through an explanation, the next step is to blame someone else, perhaps a distracting passenger or the accomplice. The bigger the stakes, the more convincing they try to be.

Often, the first reaction to a loved one's death is to place blame, whether deserved or not. Doctors and hospitals are regularly blamed for the death of a loved one. In the case of a murder or drunk driving crash, it is easy to place blame for a willful or negligent act. In the case of suicide or tragic accident, placing blame is harder, and often futile. Still, we try to do so.

As you talk about and think about what happened it is important to try to walk along healthy paths. Still, when facing this loss your initial reaction may be to hold a family member, a friend, or even yourself responsible for doing or not doing something which you feel would have prevented the death. This is frequently unjust, and nearly always unhealthy for all concerned.

Those who are accused will become targets for the accuser's frustration. Redemption and reconciliation will be difficult, if not impossible. Everything related or even unrelated to what happened will become their fault as they become a scapegoat. As they have to deal with this additional stress – perhaps even coming to believe in their own guilt – their health, self-esteem, and life will suffer from being blamed for this tragedy.

Whether blame and responsibility for the death seems to be a clear-cut case to you or not, try to be gentle with yourself and others. Try to give yourself some distance from the event before you accuse someone or hold them openly responsible. Talk to your clergy or a grief therapist in confidence before you begin condemning yourself or others for what happened.

Perhaps you are a target of this behavior, yourself. If so, you know how devastating this can be. Sometimes, people will even victimize themselves by voluntarily assuming guilt, or imagining that others blame them, despite reassurances that is not the case.

When accusations and blame like this exist, the best chance of reaching a healthy resolution lies in communicating with one another. Try to talk to those with whom your relationship has been damaged, though you may need to give them some time and distance from the death before you can bring up the subject. If the relationship is particularly strained, it may help to meet on neutral territory, with an impartial mediator, or have a mutually concerned friend present to help with the discussion.

You may find that you have to spend a significant amount of time and energy repairing the damage which has been done. Since real progress depends on the courageous and honest cooperation of both parties, you may not make any headway at all, but at least you can try to reclaim what has been lost. You can try to keep this relationship from becoming a casualty of this tragedy, too.

Healing wounds such as this can be a painful task. It is so easy to lash out in unconcerned frustration following a traumatic loss. It is easy to take a destructive road, slashing and burning a path through life, or crawling off into the shelter of withdrawal. It is not easy to talk with complete honesty about personal details, feelings, and attitudes, or to exercise the forgiveness and compassion necessary to begin the process of reconciliation with another. It is not easy, but it is often well worth it.

It is important to realize that, life being what it is, we make decisions every day. Some of those decisions probably lead us away from harm; some may lead us toward it. Most likely, all of us can remember close calls where we would have been hurt or even killed if we had been just one car ahead, or had followed our usual routine instead of deviating from it for once. The nature of our existence does not allow us to know what could have been.

What causes these coincidences? That is a question which you yourself must answer based on your personal beliefs and understanding of life. It is significant to note that while we often celebrate our good fortune when good things happen, we resist recognizing that bad things can happen, too. And sometimes, the good fortune of one means harm to another, as when a woman once missed her airline flight, allowing another person on standby to take her place. When that flight crashed, one family celebrated its good fortune while another mourned its bad.

We are only human. We cannot hold ourselves or others accountable because we didn't see into the future, didn't read someone else's mind, didn't see as well in foresight as we do in hindsight, or just flat out made a mistake. In allowing ourselves to begin to get better and maintain healthy relationships with those around us we must courageously approach guilt, blame, and accountability with a measure of compassion, kindness, mercy, and even forgiveness. This is important, not only for the well-being of those who support us, but also for ourselves.

Homicide

Homicide is the act of one person taking the life of another, but it is not as simple as that. The legal system has several categories of homicide ranging from completely unintentional, often resulting from carelessness or unfortunate accident, to the brutal and horrifying killing planned and carried out against someone willfully and with malice. Punishments for those convicted vary widely from type to type and state to state.

If you are dealing with a homicide, and here it should be noted that drunk driving crashes are considered homicides, not "accidents," it will be easy for you to place blame for what happened, especially if the killer has been caught. But, even though there may be someone whom you hold accountable, you must still live with the consequences of that person's actions.

In a homicide there are many victims, not just the one who was killed. The death of any member of our community has an effect on all, spreading like ripples in a pond, and there are many who will be affected by this tragedy. You will be aware of only a relatively close few, but nearly everyone who was touched in some way by your loved one at work, at school, and in life will be affected by this loss. It is not uncommon for these people to re-examine their lives, try to bring some good and some significance from this tragedy, or even embark on new and perhaps healthier paths and lifestyles. Since it is a crime against society, the tragic senselessness of homicide has a particular way of drawing sympathy and response from the community.

With homicide, family and friends often have to endure additional complications to their grief. These complications can include the many distractions inherent in dealing with the investigation and perhaps a trial, as well as other, more personal uncertainties related to the death.

In the aftermath of a homicide, unpredictable, intrusive, and unpleasant reminders will arise as the case develops and progresses. Some people find that this can postpone their griefwork, a situation which can have unhealthy consequences if the grief becomes linked to the outcome or progress of the case. For example, the person or persons responsible may or may not be caught; if caught, they may or may not be tried; if tried, they may or may not be convicted.

Though you may not even be aware that it is happening, allowing the success or failure of the case to affect when and how you deal with your grief can limit your progress. Try to recognize that you are dealing with separate events – the death, and the case. Your best progress may lie in your ability to deal with these events separately, as well. As difficult as it is to deal with the additional stress of the investigation, it is one of the sad realities that we must face when homicide intrudes on our lives.

Regardless of how the legal system views the death, you must come to grips with the fact that one or more people were directly or indirectly responsible for the death of your loved one.

If they go to jail, they will live forgotten, meaningless lives. Try to live yours as just the opposite.

If they are freed or acquitted instead, or paroled at a later date, you will not be able to exact revenge without committing a crime yourself. The reality is that you must let society deal with and enforce its sense of justice. If we are unfulfilled by the legal system, that is one more thing which we must learn to live through, though we may not be at all happy about it.

Sometimes, the details surrounding someone's death reveal surprising, embarrassing, or unbelievable things about that person's activities, behavior, or lifestyle if drug use, violent behavior, or other problem areas are uncovered. Friends, partners, or enemies may cast a shadow on a family's memories, and perhaps reputation. If this is the case for you, remember that no matter what details may arise, your loved one's decisions were their own. Their actions may be judged by others, *but your pain, grief, and love for them cannot be.* It is insensitive for people to try to diminish your loved one's life, or death, based on what he or she was engaged in at the time.

Often, homicide makes us fear for our own safety. This is natural and, you may find, temporary. Some people change their behavior and become more safety conscious following a homicide. Generally, this is probably not unhealthy, unless it becomes an obsession, or paranoia begins to dominate one's life.

The manner of death may be disturbing, especially if torture or other physical violation was involved. Often, we can accept the actual death better than we can accept the brutality experienced by our loved one. Again, these are things that you will have to talk through in order to come to grips with. Holding your feelings, reactions, and thoughts inside can have a serious impact on your health and your ability to function every day.

Bad dreams, overwhelming images, and unwelcome distraction and fear may be part of your life for a time. Talking about the death and what happened will be an important step in working through these symptoms. It is not morbid or macabre to want to know what occurred, see the police report, or read the Medical Examiner's report. It can actually be far worse *not* to know the details, leaving everything up to our imaginations, instead. Often, in not knowing, our imaginations can torment us with scenes which are even worse than what really happened.

Getting the most effective support following a homicide often hinges on finding people or groups with similar experiences. Since homicide is a crime against society, many of these support efforts also include opportunities to assist in prevention measures, legislative action, and victim assistance. Getting involved in these activities can bring some important significance to your loss and get you involved with some very caring people. In your involvement, you will most likely find great benefit for yourself in helping others.

Suicide

Suicide brings about particular difficulties for family and friends. Often, because of the personal nature of the death, there is a lot of blame and guilt, especially with those who were among the last to interact with the deceased. Having someone in the family complete suicide can be socially difficult and may expose the family to painful questions and uncomfortable scrutiny, or cause talk in the community. Others may not realize that, like homicide, no one can catch suicide from someone else. It is not rational for friends to avoid you, but it may happen nevertheless.

In an effort to investigate the death, the authorities may require a great deal of personal information or even challenge the survivors' integrity. This can bring additional pain if you are confronted by people who do not view the death with the same compassion as with a physical illness, accident, or homicide.

Suggestions of psychological problems may be implied following a suicide. Some may be accurate; those circulated by rumor or speculation probably will not. Our society is still very uncomfortable with psychological illness, depression, and its related effects. This can lead to a sense of shame for a family, or feeling out of place or even unwanted in social circles.

Finally, strong religious conflicts may arise. Today, among religious leaders and denominations suicide is generally treated with compassion and sensitivity. Unfortunately, old traditions and prejudices still persist. People may tell you that your loved one's act of suicide condemned them for all eternity, or something similar. The insensitivity of statements like this is baffling. Not only are these comments mean-spirited and unkind, but the people who say them simply do not know what they are talking about. They should perhaps be more concerned that they will be shown more mercy than they are showing you and your loved one.

Suicide may result from any number of long-term accumulating stressful factors such as illness, depression, drug or alcohol abuse, or other complicated choices or paths. It is not a simple or easily understood action and it is not easy for the family to bear the burden of the death.

While many of us have trouble comprehending why anyone would want to take their own life, for some, for whatever reason, it can become a consuming part of their everyday existence. You should know that those who are intent on taking their own life can be very clever about hiding it from others. There would be very little you could do to prevent someone from completing suicide if he or she truly desired to do so, and other, more certain attempts very often follow prevented or failed ones.

Feelings of guilt for you, your family, and friends of your loved one may be tough to work through, but our hindsight is always better than our foresight. If you are feeling guilty about what has happened and what you perceive as your role or responsibility in it, talk to someone who has a personal perspective on suicide. Find a support group or someone in your community who will talk with you honestly about your experience, and theirs. You will most likely find them to be very understanding as well as helpful.

Suicide rates seem to be rather stable throughout the years. However, if conditions in society or a community become more pressured, suicide rates can rise. Individuals may be at risk for suicide when entering new or stressful situations or dealing with other uncertainties in life that seem overwhelming, especially if accompanied by some form of depression.

After the death of a loved one, certain close family members may also consider suicide as a way out of their pain. Some will simply develop a lack of interest in life or their health which indirectly leads to their own untimely death. Fortunately, these thoughts begin to lessen as we find that we can and do survive the loss. Our lives begin to take shape and meaning again and, though we may develop a lack of fear when it comes to death, we will not do anything which will purposely shorten our time here.

On the other hand, those who decide to plan their suicide may begin to shut out family and friends and become withdrawn. They may begin to carefully tie up business and loose ends or start giving away their possessions. They may knowingly or unknowingly say or do things which may cause concern among their family and friends but which may not actually cause alarm.

After your loved one's death, you may be able to look back and see how the puzzle fit together – the significance of the things he or she did and said. This may help you understand the course of events, but understanding *why* may prove to be more difficult. Even when your loved one leaves behind a note, pinpointing a specific cause for the decision can be elusive.

Many suicides are associated with drug and alcohol use. Some are impulsive decisions and some are planned carefully long in advance. Research shows that the vast majority of suicides are associated with some form of depression which, while often treatable, can be a vicious and stubborn adversary. While it is difficult to categorize suicides, it seems that there are generally three purposes which are seen as being served for the one who plans and carefully orchestrates their own death. These three general patterns may serve to help you better understand the mind of your loved one.

First, it is the ultimate last word. It may be a way of actively hurting someone or making them regret something they have done or said. It is the final and ultimate exercise of control over one's life that no one can respond to. Sadly, it generally has the desired effect, creating not only grief from the loss, but also remorse and regret over unreconciled issues or decisions.

Second, it is done out of the perceived inability to face the future, the consequences of something which has been done, or life itself and the stress which accompanies it. Perhaps mounting debt; poor business or personal decisions; or fear of impending age, illness, or doom makes the future a fearful place. This future is one that they cannot or do not want to be part of, regardless of the support offered and the assurances they receive.

Third, it is done by people who feel that they have so many problems, or perhaps so much illness, that they are a burden on others and that everyone would be better off without them. The sad irony here is that everyone actually winds up being worse off due to the enormous grief which accompanies such a sad decision.

No matter what the method, the events leading up to it, or the motivation behind it, you must now work through a very complicated form of grief. Again, seeking out those with whom you can identify will most likely help you. No outcome will be perfect, for none can restore your loss, but you can make some decisions which will be more healthy than others.

You will need to take care of your own grief, that is most important right now, but you may also need to focus on those who require your support. Just as with a homicide, many people are affected by a suicide and they will have many questions. Perhaps others close to your loved one will come to you with a sincere need to understand. They may need as much information as you are willing to give them so that they may also begin to answer the question "Why?" in their own minds.

You may also find that they need reassurance that a similar job, similar stress, or other similar life choices do not make them more likely to follow the same course. Human beings can be very superstitious when it comes to this sort of connection between an event and its perceived cause. Children especially may have a hard time dealing with the suicide of a parent or role model. They may need some specific attention or professional help in order to cope with a sense of abandonment or other feelings which they have a hard time understanding.

Real progress has been seen when people pull together after a suicide, rather than letting its mystery and stigma divide relationships and pull people apart. Above all, be honest with yourself and others. Support each other with mercy, compassion, and kindness. Talk about what happened and, more importantly, talk about how you are responding to what happened. Remember the good things more than the bad, and try to bring something out of this tragedy which will memorialize your loved one and their life. That is where you and your family have some ability to control the present and the future as you live here and now.

Tragic Accident

Of all the traumatic losses discussed in detail here, tragic accident can cause the most soul-searching and be the most difficult to rationalize. Death has resulted from a seemingly senseless or perhaps random act, or a moment of carelessness or neglect. We speak of this as someone being in the "wrong place at the wrong time," or a case of "bad luck." These events seem to depend on chance more than intent and as a result often cause us to question our understanding of the world and our place in it.

The questions come fast and furious. Good things happen to good people and bad things happen to bad, don't they? Why couldn't the car have come a moment sooner, or later? How did the children know where the gun was hidden? Why wasn't she wearing her seatbelt? Why have we been struck by this tragedy?

Like other traumatic loss, accidental death comes without warning. Up until that moment, life was normal. Plans were made for the evening, tomorrow, the weekend. Now the plans have changed to include a funeral or memorial service instead. The chaos of life comes crashing down around us and we are engulfed in its storm. A hole has been ripped right through our hearts and every day we will have to walk past it and work around it as we go about our lives. This is part of the adjustment that we will go through as we learn to live with what is normal for us now.

As with the other losses discussed, tragic accident can bring deep feelings of anger, guilt, and blame. Over time, your anger and frustration will most likely begin to soften as it ages and begins to be replaced by sorrow. You may try to blame yourself or others for decisions that were made which led up to the death; however, with a tragic accident often there is no one to blame – the world has once again simply proven to be a dangerous place.

Many times, in a truly accidental event, it is additionally sad that the one directly involved in your loved one's death also becomes a victim. For the rest of his or her life the driver of the car, the operator of the machinery, the person whose action set the sequence of events into motion will have to live every day with that memory. They will relive that moment over and over. They will know that they were involved in someone's death, and most likely they will feel completely responsible. This will be a life-changing event for them, and you may find that you will become sympathetic to their pain as well.

If, however, there is evidence that this person was not acting innocently and without malice, that there was gross neglect involved, or that somehow an inappropriate decision was made that led directly to the accident, you may wind up returning to anger when you discover more details. Ultimately, you may decide that legal action is warranted either for your own personal sense of retribution, or to ensure that a similar occurrence won't happen again.

This will be a difficult decision and should not be entered into lightly. Seek wise counsel before you commit your personal and emotional resources to such a course, and make sure that you begin to deal with your grief first. Do not postpone it until afterwards. You do not know how long a legal proceeding may take, and second, your grief will become linked to the case and its success, making it that much more difficult to deal with if you are not successful in your legal efforts.

You may find that focusing on gentle acts of remembrance will bring you the most comfort as you begin to deal with this loss. Though you may be able to identify the exact series of events which led up to the fatality, knowing *how* rarely leads to an answer to the deeper and more philosophical knowledge of *why*. We are confronted by and must live with the difficult realization that not every question has an answer, not every demand a reply.

Religious Responses

Any traumatic loss, or any death for that matter, has the potential to create a strong religious or spiritual response. Accidents in particular can cause us to examine our faith and beliefs in light of what we have been taught, and what kind of support and assurance we feel we need.

When dealing with the death of a loved one, grief is a natural reaction. Grief and the loss of a loved one are unpleasant. Sometimes, the pain we feel can seem like a punishment for something in our own lives and it is not uncommon for people to feel this way, though it is neither logical nor religiously sound. It is wise to begin working with your clergy as soon as possible after a tragic accident or other traumatic loss.

If you are not a religious person, you will still need to deal with the questions and doubts which will come to mind since death can be deeply challenging to our religious and philosophical understanding. Perhaps you can find support in a group where you feel comfortable talking about philosophical issues or with someone whose insights you trust. Your understanding will probably hinge more on coming to grips with the role that chance played in the event, but that often doesn't make working through the grief any easier, or less important.

For the religious, traumatic loss often brings up questions of why protection was not provided for their loved one. They may feel that somewhere along the line an agreement has been broken or a trust has been betrayed. Even though they may believe in a life after death, the simple fact is that they are here and their loved one is not. They feel enormous pain and have questions which cannot be answered. Any explanation involving chance and bad luck will not do, and it is not uncommon to rage at God.

Don't be afraid of talking to your clergy or minister about your feelings toward God. Share your emotions with them honestly so that they can help you with your questions. If your clergy seems insensitive to, or unable to meet your spiritual, emotional, or psychological needs at this time, you may need to find someone else who can give you support in a nonjudgmental atmosphere.

If your clergy has had little or no practical experience with grief counseling, you may find that you can help them better understand the needs of those in grief as you work together. If they are willing to learn from you, perhaps there are areas you can explore together as you both work towards greater understanding of your faith and its practice.

As with everything discussed in this book, dealing with the spiritual dimension of loss must be something you come to understand for yourself. There are many books dealing with faith and loss and several very helpful ones are listed in the Bibliography in the back of this book. Typically these books are written from a Christian or Jewish perspective. In fact, there seem to be far more books dealing with how someone's faith got them through their grief in as healthy and positive a way as possible than there are books by people who work through their grief without the aid of spiritual belief.

If none of these books seems to be written from a perspective with which you agree or are comfortable, or if you are a member of a religious group which does not have widely distributed books and materials on grief and bereavement, talk to your clergy. Ask if they have any materials prepared for this purpose and talk with them about your specific needs, questions, and concerns. You may also find that books which deal with grief from a medical or psychological perspective are more suited to your needs.

For the nonreligious, the best outcome seems to lie first in finding a group of people who can provide personal care and support. These people may share a similar loss, value system, or social attraction. This is something that is usually not a problem for those who attend a church or religious gathering regularly. For those who are isolated from such a group, the path ahead may look very lonely indeed. It may require a measure of risk and courage in order to find and open up to a supportive group.

The second key seems to lie in finding some way of focusing attention on a project or purposeful activity. This can be anything which has a positive impact on society or your grief. Again, those who are actively involved with a religious community will have various ways of staying active within that group. Those living more individualized lives may need to make a conscious effort to seek out the help and activities which will benefit them the most.

Many people find faith to be an effective cushion between life and reality. It provides a way of understanding our place in the universe. Sometimes, the ability of our congregations and clergy to meet our needs and help us along this difficult path is amazing. Sometimes, however, our needs are not met and we are disappointed when we try to rely on those who are too immature in their faith to be able to helpfully put it into practice. Many of these people are often swift to offer quick-fix religious platitudes because they just don't know what to say, or what they would do in our place. This is yet another sad reality of life and loss.

Do not let anyone inhibit your grief or try to push you along faster than you are able to go because they think they have all the answers to how the universe works. Sadly, the comments of some clergy and congregation members can be the most difficult of all to bear. The untried or stoic beliefs of individuals, and even religious leaders, toward death may be at odds with the reality of your pain and emotions, especially if their experiences with grief are less traumatic than your loss. Their expectations of forgiveness, comfort, and acceptance even to the point of rejoicing may seem terribly hollow at first and even for a long time to come. By telling you how to feel and react to a loss such as this they can actually make you feel worse, guilty, inadequate, or unworthy in your own faith.

Work through your grief as *you* are able. Rely on those whose opinion and maturity you respect. Take things slowly right now. Spiritual growth often comes following a tragic loss, but like all growth, it requires energy, time, and room to expand.

We respond to various types of grief in many ways. Grief is neither simple nor straightforward. Know that what you feel is often natural and common to many. One of the remarkable things about grief is that there is much common ground. So much so that someone who has suffered a personal loss can say to us, "I know what you are going through." But, there is such wide variety to grief based on our beliefs, our personalities, and what happened that no one can say to us, "I know *exactly* what you are going through."

We are individuals and we are different. Different cultures, societies, and even communities grieve differently from others. Your grief will be a difficult and painful path for much of the way. That is simply the way grief works. For those of us dealing with a traumatic loss, it will be a lifelong journey. We hope that after a time the pain will begin to fade and we will make some good progress as we begin to restructure our lives. Throughout this process we will grieve, we will grow, and we will learn.

Now, we may have one bad day after another with some good days mixed in. We look forward to when the good days begin to outnumber the bad. That will be a major milestone for us.

Now, feelings of complete inadequacy and uselessness may be overwhelming. We look forward to when we will be able to help others in their grief by virtue of our own experiences. That will be a major milestone for us.

Now, it may be impossible to anticipate tomorrow. We look forward to the day when we can look back one year, two years, five years, ten years and more and see our progress. Perhaps we will also see all the good things that we have brought out of this tragedy, affirming life and hope in the presence of death and despair. That will be a major milestone for us.

These milestones will mark our days, and at the end, when we come to the finish line for our own lives, we will see that it was worth the enduring. We made a difference. What we did was worth doing. And we survived.

What do I do if...?

If someone tells me I must forgive the person responsible?

This is a complex issue. For people of faith who are victims of violence it can be an important and troubling one. The answer for you can only lie in your own faith and prayers, but here is how some people look at forgiveness and what it means:

- Some feel that only your loved one can forgive this act of violence. All you can do is forgive others for how their actions have affected you.

- Some are of the opinion that we as humans cannot forgive certain intentional and grossly evil acts – that we do not have the capacity or authority to do so.

- Studies have shown that engaging in true acts of forgiveness can have beneficial physical and emotional effects. It is healthy to release anger and resentment against another. It is even healthier to release one's hold over your mind and emotions by forgiving and letting go so that person can no longer influence your life. Some *restorative justice* programs have been successful in bringing peaceful resolution between victims and offenders through mediated interaction.

- Forgiveness doesn't mean declaring offenders innocent or absolving them of responsibility. It simply means they owe you a debt they cannot repay and you will no longer hold that debt as something which is due. You will no longer dwell upon it and let anger and resentment fester because of it.

- Some feel that forgiveness must be earned, or that the offender should at least show sincere repentance, remorse, or accept responsibility for his or her actions for it to be justified.

Forgiveness is a conscious decision. Arriving at a place where you can forgive can take a long time, if it comes at all. Most find that it is not a single event but an ongoing process. If this is something you feel is important, be patient. There is no hurry. Learn and grow at your own speed, not someone else's. You are *not* a bad or weak person if you do not or cannot forgive.

No matter what, do not allow someone to push you beyond what you are able to do right now, or make you feel guilty about it. If this issue concerns you, do what you can, listen to those whom you respect, then make the right decision for *you*.

Remember Me

To the living, I am gone.
To the sorrowful, I will never return.
To the angry, I was cheated.

But to the happy, I am at peace.
And to the faithful, I have never left.

I cannot speak, but I can listen.
I cannot be seen, but I can be heard.

So as you stand upon a shore,
Gazing at a beautiful sea –
Remember me.

As you look in awe at a mighty forest
And its grand majesty –
Remember me.

Remember me in your heart,
Your thoughts, and your memories
Of the times we cried,
The times we fought,
The times we laughed.

For if you always think of me,
I will have never gone.

**Debbie Ann
Walters**
First published in
Bereavement
Magazine

All in all, I'd rather take my fifteen minutes of fame in any other currency.

Letter to a Friend, February 1998

The Police and Criminal Justice System

The criminal justice system can be a complex maze of twists and turns. The police and investigating officers, prosecuting attorneys, defense attorneys, judges, and jurors are all members of the criminal justice system in our society. If you have never dealt with this system before, as quite a lot of people have not, you will find it a confusing business.

In a criminal proceeding, you as a victim do not have to hire a lawyer. Your local prosecutor's office will be working to bring about justice for a crime committed not only against you and your loved one, but also against the community. They will prosecute the case using evidence the police investigators collect.

The accused, however, is responsible for providing for his or her own defense. If the accused is unable to afford an attorney, one will be appointed, at taxpayers' expense, by the court to prepare and present the case for the defense.

The evidence presented in court most often consists of factual statements by witnesses to the crime; objects, or *physical evidence*, collected at the crime scene; and the testimony of various experts after they have examined the evidence which has been gathered. There are very strict rules regarding what kind of evidence may or may not be presented in court. While working on the case the investigators will have to be very careful about the evidence they collect and the way in which they go about it.

You may become frustrated, even angry at times, depending on how the case is progressing or how you feel you are being treated by the system. Sadly, the reality is you will still only realize a hollow victory – even if the perpetrator is caught, tried, and convicted. In this case, what has been taken from you will never be returned. This is a debt that can never be repaid.

The Investigation

In the course of an investigation, police procedures can often be difficult for the victim's family to understand or bear. The body may not be touched, moved, or removed until the scene is processed for evidence. Early on, the investigators may be required to withhold certain information from the family to ensure confidentiality. The need for the police to proceed with haste in the investigation may leave the family feeling as if they are left out or are being treated insensitively. And in some cases, notification may be delayed if the victim's identity is uncertain or if the family cannot be located.

All of these procedures can be very disturbing for the family of a victim of a violent death. But the fact of the matter is that once a body has been found the highest priorities are to find out what occurred, and who did it. Rigid procedures must be followed to preserve evidence that may lead to a suspect's capture and then to ensure a conviction. As a result, you will find yourself on the outside looking in at all the activity surrounding your loved one. Powerless to help, all you can do is observe.

If you do have questions about why certain steps are taken in the investigation, talk to the investigating officer. Most likely, there are good reasons why the case is being handled a certain way, even though it may be unsettling or unsatisfying for you.

It is a good idea to obtain a copy of the police report after the investigation is completed. Ask the investigators how and when you as a family member may go about requesting a copy. In your request, be sure to ask for any supplements which may have been written, as well. Typically, released copies of police reports are purged of names, addresses, and other personal information concerning victims, witnesses, and suspects.

In most cases, you have a legal guarantee to review the police reports once the case is complete. This does not mean that you should try to second-guess the investigation, it is simply an important record for you to keep for your own files.

Generally, a phone call to the police department handling the case identifying yourself and asking how to go about requesting a copy, followed by a simple written request is all that is necessary. Be sure to ask how long it will take to receive the report after making your request. If you do not get a timely response, some follow-up may be a necessary reminder.

It is natural for people to want to protect others from further trauma and anguish. During the initial period of your grief this may very well be a sensitive and appropriate response from law enforcement, caregivers, and even family and friends. After things settle down, however, if you have a sincere desire to see or examine documents and materials relevant to the case, it may come as a surprise to some authorities and they may be reluctant to cooperate with your requests.

This does not mean that the police have something to hide. Sometimes, these requests are simply seen as an unnecessary inquiry by the family into an official matter. Recognizing the right of victims to be informed is still a relatively new concern for the justice system and, although enormous progress has taken place in recent decades, survivors' needs are still often overlooked. Left on the outside of the system by otherwise well-meaning officials, we may need to constantly look out for our own, and our loved one's, interests.

But, even in the best cases, people often just do not realize that you are stronger now than they may think you are. The common response is, "You really don't want to know that." But we really do. They do not realize that we cannot be hurt any deeper than we have been already and that if the presentation is handled properly, knowing all the details of the incident can actually be more beneficial for us than not knowing.

We as family members are often, not always, intent to learn what happened to our loved one in those final moments of his or her life. It is the only way we can reconnect with the life that is so dear to us. It fills in a blank space in our mental record of that life. When we decide we are ready to know these details, it puts us back in control of our own lives to some extent. We are making decisions again, and that is a positive step. If officials understand this concept, they may be less reluctant to share this information with you.

Sometimes we hear and read about what happened in the media. Sometimes we hear details of the case for the first time in the courtroom. We should hear it first from those who are able to give it in the most accurate, controlled, and timely manner – the police. Police departments and victim advocates who understand and practice this know how important and valuable it is to surviving families.

Documents relating to ongoing investigations or litigation may not be able to be released immediately depending on your state's *Freedom of Information Act* legislation. Generally, though, you should expect the cooperation of the authorities in respecting your right and need for information, though you may have to convince them of your sincerity and determination to know exactly what happened to your loved one.

A typical investigation begins as the first police officers to arrive quickly assess the situation. They are trained to take appropriate action depending on what is happening when they arrive. Danger is dealt with, the injured are attended to, an investigating team is contacted, and the crime scene is secured.

The investigators begin by questioning witnesses and examining the scene. This usually involves looking for and collecting physical evidence, taking videotape footage, and taking still photographs – all of which may be presented in court.

Sometimes, the victim's body must remain where it was found for a long time until the investigators can arrive to do their work. It may not be moved or disturbed without the authorization of the Medical Examiner. Even family members are kept from approaching the victim because they will contaminate the area. Touching or moving the body may jeopardize the investigation by making certain kinds of evidence impossible to collect and this could very well affect the outcome of the case or the trial.

When the police have finished collecting evidence involving the body, it is transported to the Medical Examiner's Office, usually located in a local hospital. There it is carefully washed, x-rayed, and examined to determine the exact injuries sustained and the cause of death. The external and internal injuries to a victim can reveal valuable clues to exactly what happened prior to death. After careful examination, the wounds and injuries may be photographed or drawn on a diagram. This information will be put into a detailed report and presented at the trial.

The Medical Examiner is a highly trained physician whose job is to establish the cause of death for sudden, unexpected, violent, or suspicious deaths. In these cases an autopsy is required by law and is an important part of the investigation.

An autopsy is a surgical procedure which is usually performed by a team of highly skilled physicians. It is performed with great respect and care. Depending on the injuries sustained, an autopsy will not generally affect the family's ability to view the body in the funeral home.

If it is ordered by law, the family cannot limit the extent of the autopsy. Some states do allow the family or their clergy to request that certain religious observances be followed. If informed early enough the Medical Examiner may agree to these wishes, but *only* if it does not interfere with the investigation.

Once the Medical Examiner releases the body to the family, the funeral director is contacted and takes care of providing transportation to the funeral home for final preparations according to the family's wishes.

It is a good idea to get a copy of the Medical Examiner's report for your files also, even if you never intend to read it. Once things settle down a bit, call the Medical Examiner's Office to find out how to make your request and if there is a fee for it.

If you do want to read the report, it will be helpful to have a medical professional explain the technical details to you. If you do not have a friend or family member who is a doctor or nurse, perhaps you can discuss the report with your family physician.

It is natural to have questions about what happened, what your loved one felt, or how much suffering was involved. It is not morbid or crazy to want to know or talk about it. As you read the police and autopsy reports you may or may not find answers to these questions. If you have unanswered questions and concerns, talk to someone who is qualified to answer them and trust their expert opinion. Don't torture yourself with speculations, you will gain nothing by it.

A criminal investigation may go on for a long time. The police will be analyzing the physical evidence in the crime lab, questioning witnesses and other sources further, attempting to piece together what happened, and trying to identify the people involved and their roles. A successful outcome depends on the police not only being able to identify a suspect, but to also gather enough reliable evidence to bring that person to trial. They will be working closely with the prosecutors, trying to bring about the best result possible with the evidence they have available.

What do I do if...?

If graphic photographs will be presented at the trial?

Parents of Murdered Children has established some practical, sensitive guidelines for preparing families for what they will see in the trial. Better to view crime scene photos first in a controlled manner than to be shocked in court. You may need to convince authorities that preparation is important, so ask your victim advocate or the investigator to contact POMC if they are reluctant, have questions, or doubt the value of this.

The process is simple. Photos are placed in envelopes and numbered in order, least graphic to most graphic. In a quiet room, perhaps with your clergy present, the advocate describes the photo and hands the envelope to you. It is your choice to open it or not. Take as much time as you need. Talk about the photo and ask questions if you like. Go on to the next one when you are ready. You can stop any time. You are in total control.

When you finish, you will be able to make an informed choice about being in the courtroom for certain evidence; and if you are, you will be a far more powerful presence than if you were not prepared for this experience.

The Unsolved Case

Beyond working through the grief associated with your loss, there is the possibility that your case may be progressing slowly or is unsolved. The murderer may not be caught; if caught, there may not be enough evidence to go to trial. If your case has not yet resulted in an arrest, there is still hope. Many cases are solved months, years, or even decades after the crime. Some examples include a *cold hit* match on routine DNA testing of inmates or a suspect arrested on other charges; confessions or conversations between inmates or acquaintances; television programs featuring unsolved crimes; continuing investigations by the police department's Cold Case squad; and tips to crime hotlines or from other sources.

In some cases, a victim's family must not only live with the actual knowledge of who the killer is, but also the frustration of seeing him or her elude law enforcement or remain free due to lack of hard evidence or technicalities. In cases such as this, you should continue to communicate cooperatively with the police. Investigators may need to collect additional evidence or wait for additional criminal behavior to occur before they can act.

You cannot rush this process, but neither should law enforcement expect you to fade away or disappear. It is generally best to try to work with police cooperatively. Second-guessing their work, criticizing them publicly, or going off on your own investigation can do far more harm than good to the case and your relationship with those who may be in the best position to help you. You may have to depend on these people for a long time. Encouragement and sincere appreciation for their efforts, as with all professionals, will go a long way to keeping your relationship cordial and as productive as possible.

If you do have concerns with the way an investigation is being handled, it may be unwise to pursue a public exposure in your frustration. There are usually trustworthy official ways of dealing with the situation. Remember that investigators work on several cases at once and must balance their time between court testimony, interviewing suspects and witnesses, and analyzing the case. Their job is already stressful and the added impatience, understandable as it may be, of a family demanding progress at every turn can create more stress. Often, the investigators are as frustrated about the lack of progress in a case as the family is. The police and the family of the victim really are on the same side, though admittedly sometimes the alliance can be uncomfortable and strained. The officers may or may not be trained to be sensitive to survivors' needs. They may or may not be willing to acknowledge your questions, and there are certainly many horror stories of how families have been insensitively treated by police and in the courts. You may have to strike a balance between being assertive about your rights, and trying to minimize stress from your end to ease tensions if they arise.

Investigators learn early in their careers how important being patient is to solving a crime. Sometimes progress in a case comes quickly; sometimes it comes over a long period. You have a right to expect regular updates from investigators; they have a right to be allowed the opportunity to do their job to the best of their ability without excessive interruptions or pressure. It is not easy to stand by and watch when no progress is being made on a case, but sometimes we have little choice.

However, if you sincerely believe that an officer or investigator is not performing competently, seek an official solution – a meeting with the immediate supervising officer, for example. Express your concerns objectively, without malice or accusations. Do not burn bridges here; you may have to continue this working relationship regardless of your concerns.

In some cases, the trail simply goes cold. A suspect may have successfully eluded police or he or she may be quietly sitting somewhere in jail on other charges hoping this crime will not be discovered. You may be in for the long haul emotionally if this is the case. Pace yourself and do the best you can. Do not lose hope, but you must acknowledge the reality of the situation – the perpetrator may never be caught.

As time drags on, the investigators of your case may change or be reassigned. Additional efforts may be necessary to broaden the search with ongoing media exposure, using the Internet, or contacting and networking with other jurisdictions.

Your personal and emotional resources may become severely strained. You may find yourselves becoming public figures. You may feel overwhelmed by not only the attention but also the frustration of seeing hard work and resources leading nowhere.

This stress can lead to emotional and physical problems. Be as involved as you are allowed and as you have the strength, but take time to back away and get some rest when you need it. You can exhaust yourself with worry and activity and your personal life can suffer if you become deeply focused on the progress of the case. Don't let this situation pull apart the relationships you need most for support – those with your family and close friends. There is strength in the support of others. Pull together if you can and confront the situation in unity, not isolation.

Throughout this ordeal, you must take care of your health. Eat properly, sleep, get sympathetic support, release emotions in nondestructive ways, and stay away from alcohol and harmful drugs. All these steps will help you be as productive and as helpful as possible to those who are helping you.

At some point, police may agree that a reward may have potential or that a private investigation may be in order. There are advantages to these options, but there are also some cautions. As desperate as you are to have the case solved, you must be careful of working beyond your resources and making unwise decisions. Here are some guidelines:

• Any offer of reward will be legally binding. To make sure the details are arranged properly, get expert help and listen to that advice. Do not make unwise financial decisions out of desperation or haste. As hard as it may be, you must recognize your limitations and protect yourself and your family's future.

• To avoid scrutiny, make sure that a trusted third party or organization handles all direct control over the reward funds, donations, and disbursements. You do not touch the money.

• Do not make or publicize a decision to offer a reward without consulting investigators first. Be patient. Their professional experience and advice will be invaluable, but you must be willing to listen in order to make fully informed choices.

- Make sure you exhaust all publicly available resources first – using an established crime hotline instead of putting up your own money for a reward, for example.

- Any tips you or family members receive directly should be given to the police immediately; do not act on them yourself. There are people who may try to extort money from you or take advantage of your situation.

- If you do decide to hire a private investigator, make sure you understand your financial obligations; make sure he or she has experience cooperating with law enforcement and with this type of case; check references; and make sure your law enforcement agency is willing to cooperate with the private investigator. Avoid anyone who tries to manipulate you by guaranteeing success or criticizing the investigators to gain your favor.

- If you hire a private investigator without agreement and input from police investigators, communication problems will likely result, although sometimes this is simply unavoidable.

On another front, be careful of psychic advice or consultation. Unsolved cases can bring unsolicited leads and offers of help from professional and amateur psychics. Sometimes members of the family will want to enlist the help of a psychic in a case which has run out of leads. Many agree, however, that this is an investigative tool of questionable value.

A "psychic dream" may actually be a way for someone close to or involved with the case to keep their involvement concealed. Sometimes, unsolicited psychic leads come in when well-meaning people hear about the case and sincerely believe that they can help, though they typically provide no useable information. And sometimes, the accounts of professed Psychic Detectives who claim to have solved cases can seem uncanny and deserve serious consideration.

With the inherent potential for abusing a desperate family's trust and the lack of respected scientific evidence, it is no wonder that psychics offering to help solve a crime are viewed with skepticism or are even dismissed out of hand by officials.

Depending on the policy of the police department involved, psychic predictions may be followed-up on just as any lead, but don't be surprised if they lead nowhere. A typical pattern is for a psychic to provide many diverse predictions, creating a severe drain on police resources. And ultimately, a continuous stream of incorrect predictions will be forgotten if the police do in fact find something subsequent to the psychic's involvement.

Despite the fact that scientific tests have not yet validated psychics as a valuable law enforcement tool, and significant monetary rewards for proven psychic abilities are as yet unclaimed, we are often willing to try absolutely every possibility when we are at wits' and resources' end.

No matter how you feel about psychics, if one becomes involved in the case, for whatever reason, here are some sensible and reasonable expectations:

• The psychic must have a documented record of verifiable success with credible law enforcement agencies. Do not accept self-publicized claims out of hand. Make some phone calls. Note that claiming to have "worked" on a case does not necessarily mean he or she provided information which solved it.

• The psychic must provide reliable, specific, useable information in a timely manner which they could not get any other way through the media, friends, police, or family members.

• You should not be solicited. Accepting unsolicited help from psychics has led to many regrets and wasted resources. Many police departments even have established policies which prohibit accepting or asking for help from psychics.

• Don't allow the psychic to establish a personal or emotional relationship with the family or have any contact with them without the police present. All contact should go through the police department and *only* the police should follow-up on the psychic's suggestions.

• Likewise, any requests for personal items should be handled only by the police. *Do not* give any of your loved one's personal effects having any sentimental value to a psychic for any reason.

There is too great a risk that they will not be returned or that something will happen to them.

• Minimize the motivation of money or publicity. Avoid paying a psychic before he or she provides swift, verifiable, and accurate information. Also, never publicize the psychic's participation in the case ahead of time. Simply put, do not allow them to personally profit from your tragedy unless they produce results.

• Never make promises to the psychic and never allow them into the room of your loved one unless attended by police.

Those who claim to have legitimate psychic abilities should accept the fact that people will rely on them for results. So, if a psychic cannot produce positive results promptly, if they pressure you in any way, if they ask more questions than they answer, if they continually make excuses or gloss over incorrect suggestions as "mis-readings," if they ask for access to your personal life which would simply give them more information to use later in their predictions, or if they ask for full-payment before providing any services, these are clear and reasonable signs that you are being taken advantage of.

If any of these occur, sever relations with the psychic immediately. You have been through too much already to be led on with emotional manipulation. It would not be wise to continue to expose your family to this treatment.

Approach *all* unsolicited offers of help from outside sources such as private investigators, psychics, lawyers, and tipsters with skepticism. By all means, keep an open mind and give credit when it is due but protect yourself, your finances, and your family. The safest course is to refer all offers of help directly to the police investigators.

As awful as it is to deal with a traumatic death and an unsolved case, it is even more awful to compound that grief and stress by exposing yourself to those who may take advantage of you. Seek wise counsel from people you trust before taking any steps which could lead to embarrassment, financial loss, additional stress, or even jeopardize the investigation.

The Trials

Since a trial may or may not be in your future, only the most important points will be covered here. If you do have to prepare for a criminal trial, ask your victim assistance or local prosecutor's office for information which will help you better understand the process. Also, refer to the Appendix for books and organizations which have resources concerning the criminal justice system and your role in it.

The actual process involved in bringing the accused to trial varies from one state to another, as does the extent to which a victim's family may be present at and be heard in hearings, trials, and sentencing. If you are like many people, you will want to be present every moment of every trial and hearing involving your case. This may or may not be possible or permitted depending on the laws of the state in which the trials are held.

Fortunately, nearly all states now have victim rights legislation which guarantees certain sensible rights during court proceedings to the family of a victim. These rights vary from state to state, but they typically include: the right to be notified when and where proceedings will take place, the right to be protected from intimidation, the right to consult with the prosecutor, the right to be heard and to be present in court, and the right to restitution.

Your victim advocate should discuss these rights with you as they relate to your locality and situation so you and your family may make informed decisions regarding your involvement in the case. Your advocate should also be able to discuss how you and your family are expected to behave in the courtroom, the resources available to you during this time, and what evidence to expect at the hearings and trials you may attend. This advice will be invaluable to you as you go through this process.

Talk to your victim advocate about what type of evidence may be presented at the trial. Decide ahead of time whether you and your family will want to be in the courtroom for graphic evidence such as the Medical Examiner's testimony and crime scene photos. Most families find this the hardest part of the trial to endure, especially if enlarged photographs are shown.

You should not see and hear disturbing evidence for the first time in the courtroom. If there is a chance that you will be exposed to crime scene photos and videotapes, autopsy photos, recordings of conversations or 911 calls during the trial, your victim advocate should assist you in preparing for them.

Some cannot bear to be present when disturbing evidence is presented; others would not want to be anywhere else. This you must decide for yourself, but you must remember, no matter what you hear or see in the courtroom *you absolutely must not do or say anything* which would cause you to be excluded from participating in the rest of the trial. This is very important.

Making comments or whispering, emotional outbursts, and uncontrolled behavior from you or your family could easily result in your being ordered out of the courtroom. At the very worst, it could even be beneficial to the defense's case. *There is too much at stake here.* If you are going to participate in the trial, you must sit quietly and observe, no matter what. Your silent presence will have an enormous impact by itself. Make the most of it.

Keep your eyes and ears open. When you don't understand something, write your questions down and ask them afterwards. Get as many family and friends into the courtroom as you can, the defense most certainly will. Finally, learn as much as you can about the process, it will help you prepare for what lies ahead.

Your sense of justice right now has most likely changed dramatically from before your loss. What was once only an intellectual exercise is now a part of your daily life. You will crave justice – complete, uncomplicated, perhaps even bordering on revenge. You will not look at justice the same way ever again.

If the person responsible has not been found, you may blame the police, or you may become discouraged as the case drags on. If the perpetrator has been killed, either by self or others, you may feel robbed of your day in court. The case is closed and you have no one to focus your anger on, no trial to look forward to.

If the case does result in a trial, there are other potential difficulties. The defense attorney may try to keep you out of the courtroom by putting you on the witness list so that the jury won't see the grieving family during the trial. The trial may be *continued*, or postponed; or a hearing may be scheduled on short notice, making it hard for you to make plans to attend. You may not even find out about some hearings concerning more routine matters or procedures until they are over. Preliminary hearings may put you in the same room as the accused for the first time, or seated near his or her family. A *plea agreement* may allow the defendant to plead guilty to a lesser, more certain charge before the trial, but it often leaves victims and families feeling betrayed, even though there may have been no other choice. These things can cause a great deal of stress if they occur. You will have to ride them out as best as you can.

Participating in the trial itself may be a supreme exercise in self-discipline for you. Hearing the defendant plead "Not Guilty" may seem ludicrous to you, but remember, all it means is, "Prove that I did it." And that is exactly what the prosecution will attempt to do, but it can be a long and uncertain battle.

As witnesses testify, you may wonder why the court even bothered to make them swear to tell the truth at all. The people on the jury or their reactions may concern you. The judge may make decisions based on grounds you don't understand, or for reasons with which you do not agree. The legal terms, the motions, and the attorneys' actions or tactics may confuse you or require explanation afterwards. You may be infuriated by the attitude of the defendant and his or her family. And, depending on the case's progress, you may feel that the system has let you down. That it failed you and your loved one by holding the rights of the accused, who was present in the courtroom, over and above the rights of the victim, who was not. Participating in the drama of a murder trial can be exhausting, so try to take extra care of yourself during this very stressful time.

Find out what your rights are *before* the legal process gets started and don't be afraid to assert them. If you want to be involved, make sure the prosecutors and your victim assistance advocates know that. You may have to put your wishes in writing or fill out a form to that effect. Also, if your state allows you and your family to submit a *victim impact statement* before sentencing, begin working on it now if you wish to write one. Ask your victim assistance office for guidance in putting it together.

Another resource from Mothers Against Drunk Driving deserves mention here. MADD's Victim Information Pamphlet is a valuable guide to the intricacies of the criminal justice system. Try to read it before you begin this process.

It is a thorny path, and those who work in the justice system are often doing their best despite massive odds. Your victim advocate is there to help you understand the process and language; protect you from being exposed to intimidation; prepare you for disturbing testimony or images; and generally provide support for you, your family, and the prosecution witnesses.

Your input should be sought. Your opinion should be asked for regarding various decisions which must be made. In any case, you must try to avoid being a victim twice – first by the crime and second by the system.

It may help somewhat to remember that the criminal justice system in our society is not for the individual, it is designed by and for the community. Criminals are caught by community efforts, they are tried by members of the community, and they are sentenced and imprisoned according to community guidelines. As an individual who is personally involved, you may feel that somewhere along the line justice is not done. The simple fact is that you cannot look for comfort in a courtroom. You may find it, yes, but you can never count on it.

As the trial concludes, you will reach another milestone in your grief. This one will mark both a beginning and an ending and may bring new challenges for you and your family. Realize that nothing you experience in court will make the loss easier. Your sense of justice may or may not be the same as the judge or jury's. Though you may be able to live with the verdict, rarely is it a comfort to your sorrow and pain. You must look elsewhere for that.

What do I do if...?

If I don't understand what will happen in court?

Ask your advocate for information describing courtroom procedure and what to expect. Typically, a series of trials and hearings leads up to a criminal trial. Your advocate will be able to discuss these with you and inform you of when they will take place. Generally, in the courtroom will be the:

Judge: He or she presides over the trial and is the absolute authority. Always listen to what the judge says and obey.

Prosecutor: Presents the case for the state (your side). You may have already met him or her and perhaps discussed some issues regarding the case beforehand.

Defense Attorney: Represents the defendant. The defense attorney may be hired by the defendant or may be a Public Defender who is appointed by the state to represent the case.

Defendant: He or she will be present in the courtroom, though not allowed to speak unless addressed by the judge. Family members may also be present. Avoid them and keep cool.

Bailiff: An officer responsible for maintaining order in the courtroom and letting everyone know what is happening.

Jury: In a criminal trial, the defendant has a right to a trial with a jury. Prospective jurors will be interviewed by the attorneys before the trial starts and accepted or rejected for various reasons. A trial before a judge without a jury is called a "bench trial." Preliminary hearings do not have juries.

Court Clerk: Responsible for all clerical duties during the trial.

Court Reporter: Responsible for recording all testimony and statements during the trial. A tape recorder may be used.

Victim/You: The person, or family of the person against whom the crime was committed. A victim advocate may be with you.

Witnesses: Witnesses to the crime or related events are called to testify to what they directly observed. "Expert Witnesses" in certain fields such as medicine or firearms are allowed to give opinions based on the evidence they have examined. All witnesses are usually excluded from the courtroom until they are called, or until their testimony is no longer required.

Gallery: Anyone interested in watching the trial may attend. The judge may control the number of people in the courtroom.

The Civil Justice System

Often, as the result of a crime, a family is left with additional expenses and a financial burden that they would otherwise not have incurred had the crime not taken place. Criminal Injuries Compensation Funds help to pay for some of these expenses, but typically not all of them. In addition to these funds, a judge may order *restitution*, or repayment, by the offender during sentencing. Sadly, it is an unfortunate fact that in most cases the criminal has no assets or ability to pay a substantial fine even if restitution is ordered.

The criminal justice system works to identify people who have committed crimes against the state, determine their guilt or innocence based on the evidence, and sentence them to punishment or rehabilitation when they are found guilty. Even though the prosecutor is effectively your representative in the proceedings, it is also true that he or she represents everyone in the community. This can be an unsatisfying situation for the family of the victim if they feel left out of the process, and even when the prosecution is successful and the offender is convicted, accountability is to the state rather than the family.

However, there is a movement in the world of victim advocacy that every victim should be aware of. The criminal justice system is only one of two methods of seeking redress for a criminal offense. The *civil justice system* exists to determine if someone is *civilly* liable for injuries resulting from a crime.

In order to bring a civil suit, the victim or victim's family must retain their own lawyer. After discussing the options with the lawyer, the family may decide a civil suit has merit and begin litigation. The resulting lawsuit may result in a settlement or a trial. However, in this case, the defendant is accountable to the person filing the suit – the victim, not the state. If found liable, the defendant must pay the monetary damage award directly to the victim, assuming he or she has the assets to do so.

A victim's right to file a civil lawsuit against the perpetrator or a negligent third party exists independent from the criminal prosecution. A civil suit may be brought regardless of whether there was a conviction, or any criminal charges at all. Many people have proven in civil court that someone was "liable" for a death or injury even when the state was unable to prove the person was "guilty" of the crime in criminal court. This is because proving liability in a civil trial requires less than the "proof beyond a reasonable doubt" required in a criminal trial.

An offender does not have to be found guilty or to have been prosecuted at all in criminal court in order to be found liable for damages. Furthermore, a case against a third party may be brought if that party somehow negligently contributed knowingly, or unknowingly, to the crime and its outcome.

Victims are finding the civil court system to be an effective way of recovering expenses that are not covered by other sources. They are also recovering damages for pain and suffering, something which is generally not covered by restitution orders. Ultimately, families are holding the criminal directly accountable, and regardless of whether the offender can pay the damage award a moral victory is often greatly satisfying.

There are several disadvantages to using this system. You will be entering another trial process, this time one of your own making and requiring more active and direct input from you. You will have to engage your own lawyer, and if the defendant is not found liable, or cannot or does not pay the damage award, neither you nor the lawyer will receive payment. And finally, your state may have a statute of limitations which can limit the amount of time you are eligible to file a suit of this type.

If this is an option you would like to pursue, contact The National Crime Victim Bar Association at the National Center for Victims of Crime. Their contact information is in the Appendix. People there can advise you as to whether it may be worthwhile pursuing a civil suit for damages. Also consult the MADD brochure, <u>Selecting a Civil Attorney</u> for more insights.

Filing a civil suit is not going to be an option for every situation, but there are times when it is important to hold someone liable for criminal or negligent actions if they resulted in serious injury or death. Remember, however, do only what you have the strength to do. A very real consideration is whether this action will bring more or less stress to your life.

What do I do if...?

If I don't understand the terms used by the lawyers?

You may not understand many of the legal terms used in the trials. Some recognizable words have meanings different from everyday usage, some are very technical terms, some are Latin. Here is a glossary of a few of the words you may hear in court:

Acquittal: Finding the defendant "Not Guilty."

Arraignment: A hearing where the suspect appears before a judge, is formally accused of the crime, and enters a plea.

Bail: Upon payment of a fee set by the judge and a promise to appear in court, the suspect may remain free until the trial.

Ballistics: The science of analyzing firearms and ammunition.

Circumstantial Evidence: Evidence that is not conclusive.

Closing Argument: The final summary of the case by each side.

Continuance: Officially postponing or delaying the trial.

Conviction: Finding the defendant guilty of the crime.

Dismissal: A decision by the court not to continue the trial.

Hearsay: A statement based on information heard from another.

Indictment: The formal written accusation of the suspect presented by the Grand Jury after deciding the case has merit.

Mistrial: Ending the trial if something happens to jeopardize a fair trial or makes the trial unable to continue.

Motion: A request by either attorney that the judge make a decision on a point of law.

Noll Prosequi (nol pros): A decision by the Prosecutor not to continue with the prosecution of a case at this time.

Opening Statement: At the beginning of the trial each side presents a summary of what they intend to prove in the trial.

Plea: The defendant's formal answer to the charges.

Perjury: A witness intentionally lying under oath. Punishable.

Probable Cause: Facts that lead one to reasonably believe that the accused actually committed the crime.

Subpoena: A written order to appear in court.

Testimony: Oral evidence presented during the trial.

Verdict: The final decision of the judge or jury.

Haven't written here for a long time. Mostly growing and just living day to day. ... I am weaker than I look, but stronger than I feel.

Journal Entry, June 2000

Long-Term Grief – Living the Marathon

Out of necessity, this chapter, new to the third edition, will be the most personal of this book. It is time to talk less about the collective "people in grief," and more about how all of this has affected me over time. It is the only way to describe what the last few years have actually meant to me as an individual and what I have observed in others as our journeys intersect.

It is only now that I am able to write on this topic. I needed to put some years between me and my own personal loss before I could begin to address the issue of long-term grief. Even so, after only three years, one could hardly call this long-term.

Certainly what I experience now is no longer the crushing effect of the immediate shock of my son's death, nor is it what I think it will become as I look into the eyes of my friends who have been carrying similar burdens for decades. Their mature grief is different from mine, just as mine is different from that of my newly bereaved friends.

It is as if grief is a tiger. At first he was on the prowl constantly with razor sharp claws and fangs, ready to pounce on me without warning at any time. Now, he has aged somewhat. His weapons are duller than before and he seems to sleep more and tear at me less. Perhaps someday, he will sink into a deep but fitful slumber, never again rising to tear great chunks from my heart. Even so, he will never really leave. Like my brute of a dog lying on the floor, I will always have to step carefully around the tiger. There is no other way to peacefully coexist.

Vulnerability

I have found in the years that have passed that I am most vulnerable at times of remembrance. The word "anniversary" no longer holds a promise of celebration. Instead, holidays and birthdays, family gatherings and otherwise joyous occasions contain an undertow of sorrow. If I get caught up in it, I quickly get pulled under and wind up gasping for breath. It is ironic that the presence of an absence could be so emotionally devastating.

I have had to leave wedding receptions, sneaking away simply because I knew too much about what the future could hold for the happy couple. I have looked at a beautiful infant and my admiration was spoiled by unthinkable and unspeakable possibilities. I have shared tears with friends who have outlived their beloved spouses and children.

In all of this, I have come to realize that no one wants to know the future. Not really. It is enough for it to be revealed to us day by day. To know what would be ten years hence, or even tomorrow, would be no blessing but a curse on our ability to live today to its fullest.

Friends and acquaintances often ask me how I'm doing, but less than half a dozen will ever get a completely detailed answer. It is enough for the rest to know that I still have bad days but that I am generally doing well. Sharing more detail than that would unduly burden them. It is censored honesty, I suppose.

Then there are those golden friends; those with whom I can share my pain and wrestlings with grief openly and it will be no burden for them at all. They will nod in appreciation and recognition, for my journey retraces their steps. They know what it is like to lose someone so dear, and that is why they listen. True sympathy from such as these is like a refreshing breeze on a hot day.

Saddest of all are the faces of those who approach me when I am signing books at conferences and in an instant I know that we share an agonizing bond. There is always something in the eyes that tips me off and immediately we are no longer strangers. I know before they tell me what they are going to say. A son, a daughter, a husband, a wife, a parent – the faces are different, but we are all carrying the same burden. Our shoulders have become a great deal broader since our respective tragedies.

For those of us who seem to be getting through our bereavement by "handling it well," it is perhaps not so much that we are stoically and bravely controlling or suppressing our emotions. Rather, I think we merely learn to carefully choose the time and place where we can give them free rein for a while. We develop at least that much control. It does take some time to get to this point, unless we willfully control the uncontrollable or deny the undeniable in unhealthy ways. I see a lot of that, too.

In order to begin to process our grief we must be willing to open that door in our heart and mind that we nailed shut in our initial shock and have the courage to confront whatever we find there. A terrifying prospect, to be sure. Revisiting those memories can be dreadful. We try to avoid recounting that night at all costs. The imagined answers to our questions are perhaps more horrible than the truth, and so we leave the questions unasked and give substance to the imaginary.

Ironically, the very thing we fear most is the thing that will help us most. If we can dare approach these thoughts and memories with courage in a safe environment, with the comfort of friends, family, or professionals who are not afraid to see us at our lowest, there is hope for making good progress. These rare and supportive people are not afraid of what we might say, feel, or do. Perhaps they are even braver than we are.

It is not easy, but we must walk through this valley in order to get to the other side. Staying on this side of the valley without ever entering it is like a seed that refuses to sprout, and it produces much the same result.

I understand more fully now that grief is part of our lives. Death is part of living. To refuse to grow into it and see what it will teach us is not to grow. Like it or not, it is now part of us. Like the tiger it has come to live with us and it will not leave. To adjust, to adapt, to grow, to live again with purpose and hope – those are our goals, and I am slowly finding they are attainable.

We can actually take some comfort in this. The human race has had to deal with death ever since we became aware of it. We deal with it by grieving. It is neither a disorder, nor a disease, nor even an enemy. If we acknowledge this natural process which holds sway over our minds and bodies, we learn to deal with it as an intrinsic part of our being. Then we can know that we are approaching our loss as all those who have gone before us have, in the way that is uniquely suited to our existence.

If we as human beings are in fact specifically equipped to handle death in this way, then acknowledging our grief and making it part of our lives is the healthiest way to go. Denying grief a place in our lives works against our nature. We readily see that when people try this approach, it can lead to mental and physical complications which are unhealthy in the long run.

Two things have perhaps surprised me the most in these few years. One is the overwhelmingly wonderful people out there who are able to support us with extraordinary kindness and compassion. The other is how many people are just the opposite.

The wonderful people are truly wonderful. Many have been through similar losses. Many simply have unselfish and caring natures and precious hearts. Their capacity for kindness never ceases to amaze me. They are gentle souls and the world is a better place because of them.

The other group is a puzzle. These otherwise decent people will say the most insensitive things, or worse, will try to find some fault, sin, or reason why this tragedy happened. The assumption, of course, is that it could never happen to *them*. Some of us have gone so far as to collect their outrageous remarks and circulate them around our support groups. The strangest thing is that, though some of these people really are mean-spirited, many of them actually believe that they are saying something helpful. What they need to learn is that all they really need to say is, "I'm sorry."

I suppose the ones who are in denial that tragedy could strike at the heart of their family also are the most pitiable. At the bottom of their need to place blame on the victim or the family is fear. These Job's accusers are afraid to admit that they are just as vulnerable as I am. There must be a reason why I have been visited with tragedy, and if these people can avoid all the "mistakes," they will be magically protected from all harm.

Sadly, this is not the way the universe seems to work. If tested by the storms, their emotional fortress will prove to be nothing more than a house of cards. The rain falls on the just and the unjust alike. One cannot rationalize it away and ultimately, why it happened is far less important than what we make of it.

Between the time we are born and the time we die there is a lifetime. That lifetime may last a matter of minutes; it may last a century. No matter how long our lifetime lasts, no matter what you believe about what happens when we die, what we do between those two dates matters. It is not what happens to us, but how we respond to what happens to us that defines who we are and how we will be remembered. This is where we prove ourselves. It is either where we run a good race, or go home empty-handed. Grief is just one more race that has to be run. And, like all of life's races there are no real winners, only participants. Being in the race is the only thing that counts.

Grieving and Growing

The hardest things for me to deal with now are the weariness and the loneliness. The weariness seems to build over time. It is like chronic pain, always present and draining my energy. I can perk up for short periods and muster bursts of energy for events, but afterwards, I will need time to recover and rest. I have learned to build this into my lifestyle. Sometimes exercise seems to help; other times, it may drain the precious energy I have left and lead me to exhaustion. It varies from day to day. Perhaps someday the weariness will not be as overwhelming as it is now. I am told that this is generally the case.

The constant yearning is what is so tiring. Even if one is not obsessed with the loss, there is still the constant drone of yearning in the background. The reality is that my son is never coming back – not for the holidays, not for spring break, not for a weekend. Even though I accept that reality, it still hurts.

This yearning leads right into loneliness. It is strange to feel lonely in a crowd, but that is typical. Others tell me the same thing. Even surrounded by people we are still lonely because the one person we want to be there is absent, and they always will be. It is not an easy thing to get beyond, but I have found that the ache has dulled with time. The loneliness is not as persistent as it once was, but it is still there.

All in all, I find that for me, grief runs in cycles or perhaps waves. I describe it to others this way: From day to day there are peaks and valleys. Good days and bad days, if you will, sometimes several in a row. But what I had to get used to was smaller peaks and valleys within the larger ones, tiny changes up and down in each larger wave within the day. In a generally good day there may be some difficult moments, or some joyous ones, depending on what happens. It is the same for bad days.

These minor peaks and valleys require some adjustments in lifestyle. Emotionally, we are riding lower in the water now because of our grief. It doesn't take as much to push our heads under as it once did. We are not able to bounce back as quickly as we used to. Things that would not have bothered us before now are treacherous. This is why it is so important to stay as healthy as we can, to rest and eat on a regular schedule, and to avoid conflict and additional stress whenever possible.

As the bad days give way to more good days we can begin to relax a bit. Now, with the good days generally outnumbering the bad, I try to be more positive. It is easier to be optimistic and hopeful. That doesn't mean that I won't be set upon by another run of bad days occasionally, with the accompanying sorrows and pains, but there seem to be fewer of them now than there once were.

It is a mistake to think that people receiving good immediate care and attention when they are first bereaved will not need any more attention later. I find I need just as much support today as I did in the first days, but the type of support I need has changed. I do not spend as much time now connecting with group support resources as I do connecting with personal support. One I have outgrown, the other I have grown into.

It is natural for people's needs to change as they grow. For me and others, group support was very important early on. Now, more individualized support seems to be more effective – spending time with those who are uniquely suited to listen or advise. One way of looking at it is that my personal support system has become more self-sufficient. Later, the pendulum may swing back the other way, who can tell?

As always, changes in our lives can present complications which must be addressed. Quite frankly, when new people enter our living circle it is quite a drain to bring them up to speed on what has happened. People run into this all the time with new friends and acquaintances, new jobs, or old friends who have been out of touch. Resting in the strong, supportive friendships we already have is a great comfort.

I have also found great enjoyment in vacations or getaways where no one knows us. We tell the people we meet only as much as we want, and for a time the daily reminders and cares are washed away. We are like actors walking on the stage for an evening, content to be only who the script calls for rather than three-dimensional people with complete histories.

Holidays such as these can be an important break from day to day living, a respite from our present situation. Just as vacationing at a place that holds painful memories can be a valuable and moving experience as we journey through our grief, vacationing somewhere that holds no ties to the past can be an equally valuable break from the task set before us.

What is the most important element to survival for those of us who have been stricken by tragedy? I would have to say now that it is finding a purpose. Some find purpose by focusing on the living around them who depend on them – children, spouses, friends, other family members – those people need us around. If we begin to feel that we are not important to others, there really is very little that will keep us going. It is important to find purpose in the lives of others. It is just as important for those others to let us know that we are needed and appreciated.

Some find volunteer work to be an effective outlet for their grief. They find purpose in working with organizations and groups. Couples seem to find this an effective way of solidifying their identity. We know that tragedy has motivated the creation of many good organizations and programs. Ironically, loss has made opportunities for others possible. Death has enabled others to live. As in the aftermath of a forest fire, there are some flowers and plants which will only sprout after their seeds have been exposed to intense heat. Though all around is charred and barren, there is still life and beauty rising from the ashes.

The greatest danger for us lies in succumbing to the mindset that nothing really matters. An insidious and persistent attitude of not caring can deeply affect our entire outlook on life. It turns all the colors of the world to gray. We wither in its gaze.

It is just so easy to simply stop trying. If it were not for our children, or our spouses, or our pets, or someone who needs us here and functioning, we would be in serious trouble and the self-destruction spiral would begin in earnest. We perhaps reach our most dangerously critical point when we begin to cut ourselves off from the world – being unable to get out of bed, being unwilling to leave the house, being incapable of going to work. Prolonged efforts at isolating ourselves from others are a symptom of a deep disturbance.

When we cut ourselves off from others we have nothing to focus on but ourselves and our own problems. Then the dragons begin to emerge from the caves. Dark imaginings, self-pity, and feelings of inadequacy begin to stalk us in our pain. Ultimately, we can reach a point where we are not capable of living, and don't care if we die. If we begin to head down that slippery slope, as I have seen others do, it is imperative that we get professional help before we hit the bottom.

Living the Marathon

Long-term grief is like running a marathon. If you start out hard and fast, you will burn out. If you start slow and pace yourself, you will run a good race. Many times, just living life day to day will be enough. I often turn around and realize that I have had a good day after all; that I haven't written in my journal for months; that I am actually doing pretty well, thank you.

Sometimes anger or other strong emotions come along and I have another bad day. Sometimes loneliness is the culprit; sometimes it's just sadness. But the bad days do come and go. The good days come and go, as well.

My life didn't end that night. It began. My identity, mission, and goals have changed forever. Much of my time is now spent getting to know this new person, and learning to work with him.

I seem to do my best when I take things one day at a time and keep moving forward with purpose. I have had problems occasionally trying to do too much and I wear myself out with too much purpose. Those are the times when it is good to have someone watching out for me, reminding me to slow down and take it easy for a bit.

I am still learning from my grief. It still catches me unawares at times. I once thought naively that instead of sitting in the shadow of death, I could simply, with determination and purpose, get up and walk out of it. Shadows have edges; shadows are caused by something blocking the light. Well, I would just keep going until I emerged into the light. That's what I set out to do and I had some success. What no one told me was that the shadow *moves*. One day, I'm standing in the sunshine feeling pretty good, then the shadow creeps up on me from behind and engulfs me again. I must muster the energy to hike out again. I outdistance it for a time; it catches up. It doesn't seem to pursue me as much as our paths just seem to cross.

Someday, I hope to be done with the shadows for good. I will look back and know that I have learned much from these days. I will count myself fortunate to have met the best people I never should have had the opportunity to know – we will always share a special bond. I will be able to say that many good things have come out of this tragedy and many people have been helped. I will be able to take pride and even some joy in what has been accomplished. I will feel better than I do now, even as I feel better now than I did years ago. I will be living, not merely surviving.

And all the time, I'll be carefully stepping around that tiger sleeping in the middle of the floor...

Our Long Dark Forest

One of the things I have unwillingly learned this past month is that grief changes things. We will grow through it; we will mature through it; we will learn more about ourselves and those around us than we ever wanted to know; we will re-order our priorities. What once was of vital importance to us is as dull as mud, and what we never appreciated to its fullest we find to be more valuable than gold. Yet through it *all*, we will survive. We will get stronger, and we will find the answers for ourselves that seem to work best for us.

We are all shuffling through a dark forest together, one tiny step at a time. We hold the hands of those walking with us; we try to follow the faint footsteps of those who passed this way before us. Sometimes we stumble and fall, and we are glad that there is someone there to help us up. They help us get cleaned up and back on our feet, yet at the same time the process of getting back up simply serves to put us back on our inexorable journey again.

Once in a while we see patches of light through the canopy, and we bask in it as if we had never seen light before, for we do not know how long it will last, nor when we shall come across the next patch of brightness on the forest floor. We do not know for how many miles this forest extends. Yet through it *all*, we survive. It is a long journey; it is a fearful journey, but I am assured that it is not so dark at our destination as it seems now.

Bill Jenkins
September, 1997

It's hard to leave the sadness behind, then again, I'm not so sure that can be one of our legitimate goals right now. ... I suppose I would be spared this grief if he had never been born, but given the choice of that, or having him in my life for sixteen years and losing him, I'd take the latter every time.

Letter to a Friend, August 2000

Conclusion

You are beginning one of the most difficult processes which anyone must deal with in life. Many will come to your aid; many will rise to your support. Friends, coworkers, family, members of your place of worship, and others will become incredibly important to you now. You will learn just how vital friends, family, and faith can be in times of sorrow and pain. You will learn more about yourself and others than you ever wanted to know. You will find inner sources of strength that you never knew you had. You will become more sensitive and sympathetic to the pain and distress of others. You will grow and mature in ways that you never thought possible.

There is much to do now. Some of it will be painful; some will be frustrating; some will even be joy-filled – all of it will be important. Take what you can of these thoughts and advice and use it as best as you can. Know that you are not alone. Many have traveled this road before you and have survived. Don't give up on yourself, your loved ones, or those around you.

Ask your victim assistance program for information on topics which will become more important as you get past the first few days of this new journey. They should have literature and other resources that may be of help to you now, and in the future, to assist you in this very difficult time. Find out what help is available for you and take advantage of it.

You have my deepest sympathy for your loss, and heartfelt wishes for success in working through your grief.

Nothing can make up for the absence of someone whom we love, and it would be wrong to try to find a substitute; we must simply hold out and see it through. That sounds very hard at first, but at the same time it is a great consolation, for the gap, as long as it remains unfilled, preserves the bonds between us. It is nonsense to say that God fills the gap; God doesn't fill it, but on the contrary, keeps it empty and so helps us to keep alive our former communion with each other, even at the cost of pain.

Dietrich Bonhoeffer
Letters and Papers from Prison

What do we live for, if it is not to make the lives of others less difficult?

George Eliot
(née Mary Ann Evans)

There is good help out there. The question is,
will we have the courage to take advantage of it?

Internet Newsgroup Post, August 1999

Appendix:
Organizations and
Resources

The following resources are included here because they have been found to be directly helpful to family and friends. This list is only a starting point. As you make contact with victim service programs you will undoubtedly find other resources at the national and local levels which will also provide valuable services to you and your family.

Organizations

These organizations can be reached at the addresses and telephone numbers listed. National offices should be able to give you information on chapters and resources in your area. If the organization has an Internet address, it is given as well.

Mothers Against Drunk Driving (MADD)

MADD	MADD, Canada
511 E. John Carpenter Frwy.	2010 Winston Park Dr.
Suite 700	Suite 500
Irving, TX 75062	Oakville, ON L6H 5R7
(800) 438-6233	(800) 665-6233
www.madd.org	www.madd.ca

Contact for information on local chapters in the U.S. and Canada. MADD has a wealth of books and brochures available which are helpful not only to survivors of drunk driving crashes but also a variety of traumatic losses. More information on MADD's brochures can be found in the Bibliography.

The Compassionate Friends   TCF, Canadian National Ofc.
P. O. Box 3696   P.O. Box 141 RPO Corydon
Oak Brook, IL 60522-3696   Winnipeg, MB R3M 3S7
(877) 969-0010   (866) 823-0141
www.compassionatefriends.org   www.tcfcanada.net

The Compassionate Friends is a self-help organization for parents and family members grieving the loss of a child of any age by any reason. Bereaved families may attend local support groups where friendship, sharing, and support can be fostered. The organization has extensive resources for bereaved families and those with whom they have contact – family, friends, coworkers, clergy, and others. The group's brochures may be read online at the website or obtained from local representatives. The group has no religious affiliation. Contact for local chapters in the U.S. and Canada.

Office for Victims of Crime – U.S. Department of Justice
810 Seventh Street, NW
Washington, DC 20531
(202) 307-5983
www.crimevictims.gov

A clearinghouse of information for crime victims and victim advocates with especially useful court-related topics and a directory of victim resources.

National Organization of Parents of Murdered Children, Inc.
100 East Eighth Street, B-41
Cincinnati, OH 45202
(513) 721-5683
(888) 818-POMC
www.pomc.org

Originally organized to support parents grieving the loss of a murdered child, the focus has rapidly broadened to include anyone grieving the loss of a loved one due to violence. Contact for local chapters. Brochures available from POMC are listed in the Bibliography.

National Center for Victims of Crime
2000 M St., NW; Suite 480
Washington, DC   20036
(202) 467-8700
Helpline: 1-800-FYI-CALL
www.ncvc.org

Contact for information on local and national victim rights issues. Their website contains a wealth of supportive information for victims and victim advocates. NCVC has many valuable sources of information covering a wide variety of topics and crime victim issues.

National Organization for Victim Assistance (NOVA)
510 King St.; Suite 424
Alexandria, VA   22314
(703) 535-6682
1-800-TRY-NOVA
www.try-nova.org

Contact for information on finding local victim resources.

American Association of Suicidology
5221 Wisconsin Ave., NW
Washington, DC 20015
(202) 237-2280
www.suicidology.org

A clearinghouse for information and resources regarding suicide, its prevention, and impact on survivors.

The Dougy Center:
The National Center for Grieving Children and Families
P. O. Box 86852
Portland, OR   97286
(503) 775-5683
www.dougy.org

Support and resources for children dealing with grief and loss. Contact for information on support in your area.

Center for Loss and Life Transition
3735 Broken Bow Road
Fort Collins, CO 80526
(970) 226-6050
www.centerforloss.com

The Center has exceptional resources for grieving adults, teens, and children. Contact them or visit their website for available books and materials, seminars, and services.

Murder Victims' Families for Human Rights
2161 Massachusetts Ave.
Cambridge, MA 02140
(617) 491-9600
www.murdervictimsfamilies.org

An organization of murder victims' family members devoted to restorative justice and human rights in the justice system.

The National Hospice Organization
1700 Diagonal Road; Suite 625
Alexandria, VA 22314
Help line: 1-800-658-8898
www.nho.org

Information on locating hospice services in your area. While hospices generally address long-term illness and terminal care, they are required to have bereavement programs that are free of charge and open to the public. A local hospice program should have a list of a variety of reliable resources including grief therapists, support groups, bereavement camps for children, and other resources that may be helpful to you.

Bereaved Families of Ontario
36 Eglinton Avenue West, Suite 602
Toronto, ON M4R 1A1
(416) 440-0290
www.bereavedfamilies.net

Information on grief and bereavement with extensive Canadian resources.

Internet Resources

There are many resources available on the Internet for your use. There are *webpages* dedicated to helping the grieving, *chatrooms* where you can have conversations with others in real time, and *bulletin boards* where you can post messages which others with similar interests can read and respond to. Below are some Internet resources that should get you started.

Counseling for Loss and Life Changes
www.counselingforloss.com

GriefNET
www.griefnet.org

alt.support.grief
USENET newsgroup devoted to grief and loss

GROWW – Grief Recovery Online
www.groww.com

William Jenkins Memorial Website
The story of William's murder, which led to the creation of this book. Many other features and links to other sites on the Internet.
www.willsworld.com

Living With Loss
www.livingwithloss.org

Victim Assistance Online
www.vaonline.org

About.com
www.dying.about.com

Death and Dying Grief Support
www.death-dying.com

After I've Gone

After I've gone I will still be with you.
You will see me in all the sunrises,
Saying, "Good Morning" to you.

You will hear me when the birds sing,
Singing, "Hello" to you,
And cheering you through the day.

You will feel me during the cold winter months,
When the snow falls quietly,
I will be saying, "Isn't it beautiful?"

I will be with you during Autumn,
As the leaves change colors and fall,
I will be with you watching silently.

I will be with you when the moon is full,
I will place the stars for you,
So you can reach up and almost touch them.

When a soft breeze blows across you,
It will be me touching you,
And kissing away your tears.

As the rain falls and lightning flashes,
It will be me playing a song for you,
A song of courage and of strength.

And you will see me in the sunsets,
Saying "Goodnight my love."
After I've gone, I will still be with you.

Author Unknown

*I am at my best when I am not trying to deal with
the grief. As if letting go of something actually draws
us closer in. Floating on the quicksand, as it were.
Relax and all things will come.*

Journal Entry, January 1998

Annotated Bibliography

This is a short annotated list of books that have been particularly helpful to many in their grief. Many books have been written on the various complexities of grief and loss. Some are more helpful than others; some are easier to understand than others. You will probably find that the most helpful books deal as closely as possible with your situation and are written by people you can identify with.

Many of these titles may be found in the "Self-Help" and "Inspiration" sections of most major bookstores. If your local bookstore does not have a title in stock, a copy can usually be ordered and obtained in a few days. Your local public library should also have resources available for your use.

It is easy to spend a lot of money on books. Before you buy, first check the table of contents to see if it addresses the needs of your situation. Some books pay special attention to traumatic loss, while others are more helpful for terminal illness or age-related death.

The technical language used in some books written by medical professionals can be difficult to understand, so check the text for readability. Books by survivors of loss can be very helpful as they share their survivor experiences and assurance that you are not alone in your grief. Collections of inspirational works are valuable as we ponder our loss and its effect on us.

The WBJ Press website at *www.willsworld.com* contains all of these books and more in a unique online bibliography which will be occasionally updated as new resources become available.

Books

Bozarth, Alla Renee, Ph.D. *A Journey Through Grief.* Hazelden: Center City, MN, 1990.

Gentle advice, reflections and inspirational thoughts on grief and grieving.

Bramblett, John. *When Good-Bye is Forever: Learning to Live Again After the Loss of a Child.* Ballantine: New York, 1991.

Written following the tragic death of his youngest child. An examination of faith, life, and death by the author, with helpful contributions by his wife and children.

Brown, Laurie K. and Marc Brown. *When Dinosaurs Die: A Guide to Understanding Death.* Little, Brown and Co.: Boston, 1996.

Dinosaur children learn about death and dying in a gentle and informative manner. Very educational, generously illustrated, and appropriate for elementary and middle school ages.

Buscaglia, Leo, Ph.D. *The Fall of Freddie the Leaf: A Story of Life for All Ages.* Slack: Thorofare, NJ, 1982.

A parable about death that can be useful in talking to young children. Suitable for reading to elementary school ages.

Dobson, James. *When God Doesn't Make Sense.* Tyndale: Wheaton, IL, 1993.

A Christian view of tragedy, suffering, and loss.

Emswiler, Mary Ann, M.A., M.P.S., and James P., M.A., M.ED. *Guiding Your Child Through Grief.* Bantam: New York, 2000.

A valuable and very practical book on helping children grieve and the family dynamics surrounding the death of a loved one.

Fahy, Mary. *The Tree That Survived the Winter.* Paulist Press: New York, 1989.

An encouraging parable on the hardships of life and the hope which endures through long, dark, difficult times. Suitable for children and adults.

Ginsburg, Genevieve Davis, M.S. *Widow to Widow.* Fisher: Tucson, AZ, 1999.

A practical guide filled with valuable advice and information for widows written by one who has been through it herself. A useful and thorough resource.

Graham, Billy. *Death and the Life After.* Word: Dallas, 1987.

A discussion of the spiritual dimensions of death by one of today's most trusted theologians and evangelists.

Grollman, Earl A. *Talking About Death: A Dialogue Between Parent and Child.* Beacon Press: Boston, 1991.

Rabbi Grollman is a highly regarded grief therapist. Of his many books on grief and bereavement, several, like this one, specifically address talking to children and teens about death.

Hickman, Martha Whitmore. *Healing After Loss: Daily Meditations for Working Through Grief.* Avon Books: New York, 1994.

A year's worth of thoughts and meditations on grief and loss.

Hipp, Earl. *Help for the Hard Times: Getting Through Loss.* Hazelden: Center City, MN, 1995.

A book specifically for teens discussing issues of grief and loss in a frank and helpful manner.

Holtkamp, Susan, Ph.D. *Grieving With Hope.* Franklin-McKinsey, 1995.

A touching resource which honestly addresses the issue of suffering, death, and hope with compassion and sensitivity from a Christian perspective.

Kelley, Patricia. *Companion to Grief: Finding Consolation When Someone You Love Has Died.* Simon and Schuster: New York, 1997.

A series of helpful letters from the author, who is a grief therapist, to her brother-in-law following the death of his wife.

Kight, Marsha, ed. *Forever Changed: Remembering Oklahoma City, April 19, 1995.* Prometheus: New York, 1998.

A compilation of eighty-one letters, stories, and first person accounts of the Oklahoma City bombing. An inspirational, sobering, and rich testimony to the victims and survivors.

Kushner, Harold S. *When Bad Things Happen to Good People.* Avon: New York, 1983.

A best-selling and widely acclaimed book about religion, death, and suffering by Rabbi Kushner.

Lewis, C. S. *A Grief Observed.* Bantam: New York, 1983.

An uncompromisingly honest personal journal examining faith and grief following the death of Lewis' wife. Published in the early 1960's, it is one of the first books ever published on grief and bereavement, and is still one of the best.

Lord, Janice Harris. *No Time For Goodbyes.* 4th ed. Pathfinder: Ventura, CA, 1991.

This book is available in your local bookstore and also from MADD. Although its primary focus is alcohol related car crashes and fatalities, it is a must-have book for anyone dealing with grief, traumatic loss, and the justice system.

Manning, Doug. *Don't Take My Grief Away From Me: How to Walk Through Grief and Learn to Live Again.* In-Sight Books: Oklahoma City, OK, 1999.

Also reprinted by HarperCollins as: *Don't Take My Grief Away.* An easy to read, practical book on dealing with a death in the family, how to make the necessary decisions, and enduring the natural grief that follows. The author's remarkable insights and years of ministerial experience, combined with an easy to read style are a welcome feature of his books. Other books and materials for grieving families and caregivers by Doug Manning on grief and bereavement, including some superb materials on helping children and teens, are available from In-Sight Books, P.O. Box 42467, Oklahoma City, OK 73123. The Internet website is *www.insightbooks.com.*

McCracken, Anne and Mary Semel, eds. *A Broken Heart Still Beats: After Your Child Dies.* Hazelden: Center City, MN, 1998.

A beautiful and extensive collection of short essays and inspirational writings on the loss of a child. A valuable long-term resource for the bereaved parent.

Mellonie, Bryan and Robert Ingpen. *Lifetimes: The Beautiful Way to Explain Death to Children.* Bantam: New York, 1983.

Accompanied by exquisite illustrations, the simple story is easily understandable by very young children and early readers.

Rando, Therese A., Ph.D. *How to Go On Living When Someone You Love Dies.* Bantam: New York, 1988.

A thorough examination of the effects of death on a family, this book deals with the many different circumstances and relationships involved in the loss of a loved one. An excellent book with a superb bibliography and list of resources listed by type of loss.

Schiff, Harriet Sarnoff. *The Bereaved Parent.* Penguin: New York, 1978.

A thorough discussion of bereavement and grief written following the death of her son.

Silverman, William B. and Kenneth Cinnamon. *When Mourning Comes: A Book of Comfort for the Grieving.* Jason Aronson, Inc.: Northvale, NJ, 1994.

Wise counsel on dealing with death and grief. The authors are a congregational rabbi and a clinical psychologist.

Staudacher, Carol. *Beyond Grief: A Guide for Recovering from the Death of a Loved One.* New Harbinger: Oakland, CA, 1987.

An excellent, practical, and thorough book on the effects of grief from various causes. This book may seem overwhelming at first glance, but read chapters 1 and 2 first, then skip to the chapter which most closely deals with your type of loss. Later, you may want to read the rest. Good chapter on the criminal justice system.

Strommen, Merton P. and A. Irene Strommen. *Five Cries of Grief: One Family's Journey to Healing After the Tragic Death of a Son*. Augsburg: Minneapolis, 1996.

An insightful personal account of grief and loss. The authors do an especially good job of boldly confronting the spiritual dimension of death and sudden loss. This would be an excellent study resource for church-based support groups.

Tatelbaum, Judy. *The Courage to Grieve*. Harper and Row: New York, 1984.

The author's brother was killed when she was a teenager. Now a psychotherapist, she combines her experience with her training in an effort to provide others with a path for their grief.

Viorst, J. *The Tenth Good Thing About Barney*. Athenium: New York, 1971.

A story for children and early readers about a little boy who comes to understand mortality following the death of his cat.

Wolfelt, Alan, Ph.D. *The Journey Through Grief: Reflections on Healing*. Companion Press: Fort Collins, CO, 1997.

A highly acclaimed book on grief and the needs of the grieving. Dr. Wolfelt has written several other helpful books on grief and loss, as well. Contact Bereavement Publications at the address below for a list of available titles and ordering information.

Wolterstorff, Nicholas. *Lament For a Son*. Eerdmans: Grand Rapids, MI, 1987.

Personal reflections and journal entries written following the death of the author's son in a mountain climbing accident.

Magazines

Bereavement Magazine
Bereavement Publications
4765 North Carefree Circle
Colorado Springs, CO 80917
(888) 604-4673
www.bereavementmag.com

A beautiful magazine filled with authoritative articles on grief and inspirational messages of hope. Also a full line of books and support materials on grief, loss, and bereavement including those by Sue Holtkamp, Ph.D., and Dr. Alan Wolfelt, Ph.D.

MADDvocate Magazine
MADD National Office
511 E. John Carpenter Frwy. Ste. 700
Irving, TX 75062
(800) 438-6233
www.madd.org

A magazine full of insight and inspiration, not only for victims and survivors of drunk driving crashes, but also anyone mourning a traumatic loss. Complimentary copies are sent to advocates and victims of all crimes upon request.

Brochures

Mothers Against Drunk Driving

The following is a list of brochures available through Mothers Against Drunk Driving that can be helpful to those suffering other types of traumatic loss as well. Contact the national office or your local chapter for ordering information. Your victim assistance office may also have these in stock. Also note that the complete text of any MADD brochure may also be read online at their website, *www.madd.org.*

Victim Information Pamphlet Explaining the criminal justice system

Financial Recovery After a Drunk Driving Crash

Selecting a Civil Attorney

Your Grief: You're Not Going Crazy

Will it Always Feel This Way?

Helping Children Cope With Death

Straight Talk About Death For Teenagers

We Hurt Too: A Guide for Adult Siblings

Men and Mourning: A Man's Journey Through Grief

Loss, Pain, and Healing A parent's guide to grief

How Are You Feeling? A teen's guide to loss, grief, and healing.

Unique Grief For non-family bereaved victims

Parents of Murdered Children

Brochures available from POMC are being used by victim assistance programs everywhere to help people deal with the loss of a loved one. These brochures may be available from your local victim assistance office, or they may be ordered from POMC. Visit their website at *www.pomc.org.*

Sorrow of Siblings

Inner Grief of Men

Path Through the Criminal Justice System

Thanks for Asking (A book of poetry and essays by survivors)

This is my identity now. The father of a sixteen year-old murder victim. All significant events in my life will now be referenced to August 12, 1997. All my writing, speaking, music, creativity, and everyday work will somehow be infused with the events of that tragic night.

Victim Impact Statement, February 1998

Victim and Witness Rights

The following victim and witness rights are included in a proposed amendment to the United States Constitution. Similar victim rights legislation has already been enacted in a majority of states. Consult your local prosecutor's or victim assistance office to determine what victim and witness rights are available to you in your particular locality.

`Section 1. Each victim of a crime of violence shall have the rights to reasonable notice of, and not to be excluded from, all public proceedings relating to the crime—

`to be heard, if present, and to submit a statement at all public proceedings to determine a release from custody, an acceptance of a negotiated plea, or a sentence;

`to the foregoing rights at a parole proceeding that is not public, to the extent those rights are afforded to the convicted offender;

`to reasonable notice of a release or escape from custody relating to the crime;

`to consideration for the interest of the victim in a trial free from unreasonable delay;

`to an order of restitution from the convicted offender;

`to consideration for the safety of the victim in determining any release from custody; and

`to reasonable notice of the rights established by this article.

Psalm 23

The Lord is my shepherd, I shall lack nothing.
He makes me lie down in green pastures,
    he leads me beside quiet waters,
    he restores my soul.
He guides me in paths of righteousness
    for his name's sake.
Even though I walk through the valley of the shadow
    of death,
    I will fear no evil, for you are with me;
    your rod and your staff, they comfort me.
You prepare a table before me in the presence of my
    enemies.
You anoint my head with oil; my cup overflows.
Surely goodness and love will follow me all the days
    of my life,
    and I will dwell in the house of the Lord forever.

New International Version

The only way not to hurt in this world is to not love others. If you don't love, you can't be hurt. Make your choice. Love others and have your heart ultimately broken, or love only yourself and have your heart unbreakable and atrophied beyond use.

How to Help a Friend in Grief

Journal Entry, March 1998

Your friends will be concerned about you and they will want to help in any way they can. However, our society has little real experience with grief and friends may be at a loss for what to say or do. They will be dealing with their own anguish, pain, and disillusionment with the world, as well. When people say terribly insensitive things they are generally not trying to be unkind, they simply have little or no experience with consoling someone in grief.

In order to provide some gentle and practical education to your friends, the two following pages are designed to be easily reproduced to distribute to them. Copy these two pages as often as you need to help others understand how they can better support you. Your friends will find that as they learn more about traumatic loss they will be better able to help you and others.

You have unwillingly become a member of a club that no one wants to join. Its members are amazing people. We are survivors in the best sense of the word and you will find that you can be a survivor, too. Take strength where you can. Give strength when you are able.

Two things will be more valuable than anything else: *You must allow yourself to get better,* and *you must find ways to bring good things out of this tragedy.* If you can do these two things, you will make good progress. You will not be perfect, you will not be just like you were before, you will not be without some lingering pain. But, the wounds *will* begin to heal, you *will* begin to get better, and you *will* be able to function more fully in what is now a new level of "normal" for your life.

How to Help a Friend in Grief

As much as we would like to avoid unpleasantness in our lives, sometimes it is inescapable. Instead, we must learn how to grieve in healthy ways and work through our difficulties. If you are wondering what you can do to help a friend who is in intense mourning, here are some suggestions:

- Recognize that we all grieve at our own pace. Some progress rather quickly, some move very slowly. We never move at the speed that others think we should. Help us take one day at a time.

- Keep us company and be there for us. You don't need to say anything profound or do anything earthshaking. Often, your greatest help is your quiet presence and simplest deeds.

- Make suggestions and initiate contact and activities. It is important for you to respect our privacy and give us some time alone, but we also may not have the energy to structure our lives right after a traumatic loss. We may have to rely on others to think of things that we don't know to ask for.

- Provide a safe environment for us to show strong emotions. It may be very painful, but it can be of enormous help.

- Help us remember good things. Tell us your memories of our loved one as you listen to us tell you ours. If we begin to show our emotions outwardly, you have not upset us, you have simply enabled us to be a bit more open in your presence.

- Be there after the first wave is over. Make the effort to call, to come by, to help us out six months and even a year down the road. Crowds may be difficult for us. Shopping and holidays will be overwhelming. Offer your help. If we're not up to a visit we'll let you know, but let us know you remember and are there for us.

- Listen to us. We need to tell our story over and over in order to process our grief. We may even say outrageous things. Don't judge us by what we say or how we feel. We have a lot to work through, and in time we will come to the answers that are right for us.

- Be careful of clichés, religious platitudes, or easy answers. You may not be able to help us with certain issues right now, so don't be too quick to share your opinions if we say something you don't agree with. We need time to work things out on our own.

- Be sensitive to our needs, be patient, have confidence and believe in us. We will get better, we will experience healing; but it will take some time, and it can be rough going for much of the way.

- Be on the lookout for destructive behaviors. Traumatic loss can lead some people into depression, alcohol or drug abuse. We may need you to keep an eye on us while things are especially tough.

- Help us find humorous diversion. Laughter is good medicine.

- Be willing to do difficult things with us. We may need someone to sit with us in court; we may need a safe place to rage; we may need help with the funeral or afterwards. There may be some hard times ahead and facing them alone can be terrifying.

- Help us find ways to bring good things out of the bad. It is important that our loved one be remembered and memorialized.

- Find out about grief. Read some of the books that are available. The more you know, the better able you will be to help us.

- Help us to find support and inspiration. Often, a poem or song will speak to us in ways that no one else can. Also, talking to someone who has survived a similar loss can help us realize that we are not alone in our grief.

We have to go through this valley in order to get to the other side. Dealing with grief cannot be avoided or postponed. Grief can make relationships difficult and you may get frustrated with us or feel uneasy around us. But please remember that now, more than ever, we need the caring and patient support of our friends and family. Help us get through this as well as we are able. Your true friendship and companionship, your kindness and patience can help us get our lives back together.

We will experience some level of grief over our loved one's loss *for the rest of our lives.* Some days will simply be better than others. One day, we hope to reach a point where our good days outnumber the bad. That will be a major milestone for us.

Thank you for being here for us.

to distribute to your friends and family.

Author's Note

After being notified of the shooting death of my sixteen year-old son late one night in August 1997, I came to realize several important things. One is that tragedy can strike anyone, anywhere, at anytime, and requires no special qualifications or application process. Another is that my family and I desperately wanted some guidance through the first days of our loss, but none seemed to be available which could give us the help we needed. As a result, we muddled through as best as we could, as most people do, with some successful and some not so successful decisions being made.

After meeting the very fine people in our local Victim/Witness Program some days later and attending the victims of homicide support group which the program sponsors, we compared notes and came up with a solution. With input from the group and others, I would write a book that could be given to families during death notifications. This book would not answer every question, nor would it be an exhaustive study of grief. Instead, it would be a handbook to get people through the first days, help them understand what was happening to their bodies and minds, and inform them of what to expect until more resources became available. Most importantly, it would be easy to read and understand so that it would be helpful to as many people as possible. The overwhelming success of that first effort made later expanded editions possible.

One of the things I decided the very first day after William's death was that I wanted only good things to come out of this tragedy. I can now say that there are *many* good things that outnumber this one bad thing. And though I would trade them all to have him back with us safe and sound, it is my hope and prayer that this book will be one more triumph of good over evil and order over chaos, and that it will in some small way help you as you begin your walk with grief.

I wish you peace,

Bill Jenkins

Father of William Benjamin Jenkins (1980-1997)

"Goodnight sweet prince, and flights of angels sing thee to thy rest."
Hamlet Act V, Scene 2

Acknowledgments

This book was initially developed with input from the Henrico County, Virginia Commonwealth's Attorney's Victim/Witness Assistance Program. The author would like to thank the people who collaborated or contributed in some way to make this book possible:

The Victim/Witness Program advocates who have lent their inspiration and encouragement, their experience, and their years of professional expertise in making significant contributions to the creation of this much-needed work:

Shelly Shuman-Johnson, Director
Nikki Lewis Johnson, Assistant Director

The members of the Henrico County Homicide Survivors Support Group who have lost loved ones to violent crime:

Lonnie and Louise Butler .... Patrick J. Butler

Jim and Irene Dixon .... James R. Dixon

Ken Farmer .... William McCalley "Calley" Farmer

Bill and Rita Godsey .... Rebecca Godsey

Tena Gregory .... Sylvia C. "Bootsie" Gregory

Katherine Hedian .... William Benjamin Jenkins

Vance and Francine Horne .... Vance Michael Horne, Jr.

Rev. David and Jeannie Knight .... James Edward "Jamie" Knight

Special thanks to my wife, Jennifer Bishop-Jenkins, also a murder victim's family member, and the others who have contributed to and reviewed my research: Beth Smith, *Nelsen Funeral Home*; Professor Margaret Duckworth, *Virginia Union University*; Sue Holtkamp, Ph.D., *Something More Bereavement Programs*; Jean Lewis, *The National Organization of Parents of Murdered Children*; Jeff Dion, *National Center for Victims of Crime*; Ron Gospodarski, *Bio-Recovery Corp.*; my Internet friends; and the many people and groups who have created supportive materials to help me and my family.

A heartfelt personal thanks to two very special people: author Patricia Cornwell (www.patricia-cornwell.com) for all the support, and singer/songwriter Susan Greenbaum (www.susangreenbaum.com) for all the great songs. William is indeed "One More Angel."

In helping me, you have made it possible for me to help others, and so, William's legacy continues. Thank You.

Notes:

Contact Numbers

Emergency **911**

Police Non-Emergency
and Information . . _____

State Criminal Justice
Services Department . _____

Local Prosecuting
Attorney's Office . . _____

Local Victim
Assistance Office . . _____

Local Department of
Mental Health . . _____

Family Doctor . . _____

Investigating Officer's
Name and Number . . _____

_____

Funeral Home . . . _____

Other Important Numbers and Notes:
_____
_____
_____

ORDERING INFORMATION

SINGLE COPIES:

Call In-Sight Books' Toll-Free Order Line: 1-800-658-9262

What to Do When the Police Leave is available through any bookstore. If it is not in stock, do not hesitate to ask for it.

*BULK DISCOUNTS FOR ORGANIZATIONAL OR
JURISDICTIONAL USE:*

Please contact the publisher at the address below to request a bulk discount order form:

Order Dept.
WBJ Press
315 Lockwood Ave.
Northfield, IL 60093
e-mail: wbjpress@willsworld.com

Bulk discount pricing and order forms are also available at the WBJ Press website, **www.willsworld.com**

What to Do When the Police Leave is distributed to the book trade by:

In-Sight Books
P.O. Box 42467
Oklahoma City, OK 73123
Phone: 1-800-658-9262
Fax: (405)-810-9504
e-mail: orders&info@insightbooks.com
website: www.insightbooks.com